The Wanderer

Sarah Elizabeth & Ron Whitehead, Cherokee Park 2007
photo by Christian Hansen

Published in Heaven Books
for The Global Literary Renaissance
Louisville, Kentucky USA
Sarah Elizabeth, President/CEO

The Wanderer
by Ron Whitehead
Copyright © 2007 Ron Whitehead
All Rights Reserved.

First Edition, First Printing – October, 2007

Special Thanks to Sarah Elizabeth for support and participation in every aspect of the production of this book. Thanks also to all the photographers whose names, when known, are included with each photo: Christopher Felver, Jeremy Hogan, Xavier Noel, Velvet Woosley, Christian Hansen, Reginald J. K. Price, Valerie Downes, James Walck, Greta Whitehead, Charlie Coddington, Sarah Elizabeth, and others. Thanks also to Foster Dickson, Annalisa Papaleo, Jordan Green, David Minton, Casey Cyr, to William S. Burroughs for the interviews/articles, to Bob Holman for the poem, to Gui Sedley Stuart and Sarah Elizabeth for the poems and everything else. All contributors retain all rights to their own work. I appreciate the inclusion of their work in my book. Thanks to all the publications in which many of these works previously appeared. Thanks also to everyone I have worked with, over the many years, many of whom are mentioned/shown in the poems, stories, articles, interviews, photos included in this book. I am eternally grateful. Your ancient friend, Ron.

This book may not be reproduced in whole or in part, or transmitted in any form, by electronic or mechanical means, including information storage or retrieval systems, without written permission from the author and the publisher.

Front cover photo of Ron at Yosemite, waterfall, by Christian Hansen.
Back cover photo of Ron at Yosemite, roots, by Frank Messina.

All layout, graphic art, & design by Sarah Elizabeth.

ISBN: 978-1-60458-066-2

Printed in the USA
Ron Whitehead, AHA
www.tappingmyownphone.com

The Wanderer

Ron Whitehead

Published In Heaven Books

CONTENTS   The Wanderer

1
fields of purple morning glories

2   For My Children, Now Grown
3   fields of purple morning glories
5   love on a rainy day
6   My Beautiful Mutant
7   To Ballard to the wilderness we go
8   Dream
9   Your Breath
10 Christmas, the old ways, and you
11 old veins
13 I Strive No More
14 geothermal piano: 13 Grandmothers and Sarah do the Sun Dance, with wild horses

2
from Kentucky he came

18 Old Blue Got Run Over By A Coal Truck On Christmas
19 The Sound of Falling Snowflakes
21 Moxley & Eirene: Moonshine King Burgoo Queen
25 Searching For Abraham Lincoln
31 The Dance: a choral, orchestral, song poem
37 lost poem: intimations

3
driving 100milesperhour on Bardstown Road
with Allen Ginsberg

40 On First Reading Jack Kerouac's ON THE ROAD: Down & Out in Kentucky: Part VII: For Madmen Only
42 Kerouac's Daughter
43 Without Blinking: Zen & The Art of Driving 100milesperhour past Mayor Abramson & others from Twice Told Coffeehouse on Bardstown Road to the airport
    Part IV: Down & Out in Kentucky
    Allen Ginsberg: The Bridge
45 Calling The Toads: The Antinomian Fire This Time

51 ASHEVILLE: for Allen Ginsberg
54 Deep Appreciation by Bob Holman
55 Harold Maier Is A Hero Of Mine
57 From Hank Williams Grave to Insomniacathon 2003
61 Searching For David Amram
66 closing time
68 From Jack Kerouac's Grave to Forecastle 2006

4
from Italy & Alabama to Kentucky & Beyond

74 An interview with Ron Whitehead by Jordan Green
82 An Interview with Ron Whitehead by Annalisa Papaleo
89 An Interview with Ron Whitehead by Foster Dickson
103 An Interview with William S. Burroughs by Ron Whitehead
113 Calling The Toads

5
i refuse

116 i refuse
120 This Is a Metaphysical Poem
121 A Prayer: after Burroughs
123 Dreams Memories Visions by Gui Sedley Stuart
127 Gimme Back My Wig: The Hound Dog Taylor Hunter S. Thompson Blues
130 I Found Myself in Emptiness
131 virtual photons we: zero signature
133 I Will Not Bow Down: global version

6
Creative Marriage

140 Creative Marriage

7
The Hunter S. Thompson Blastoff is Decadent and Depraved

144 en route to Owl Farm
145 Dr. Hunter Shaman Thompson is Dead

149 The Hunter S. Thompson Blastoff is Decadent and Depraved by Ron Whitehead and Sarah Elizabeth

8
Can Art Matter? Published in Heaven: Blood Filled Vessels

160 Can Art Matter? Published in Heaven: Blood Filled Vessels

9
Literary Kicks

168 Literary Kicks: Who is Ron Whitehead? by David Minton
177 The World Ambassador of Poetry (English & Italian text) by Annalisa Papaleo
188 Watching With a Thousand Eyes by Casey Cyr
195 Alfama old Lisbon Portugal February 2007

10
The Wanderer

202 Riding With Rebel Jesus, The Wanderer

11
bonus track

12
hawk and crow

232 hawk and crow: alchemical sunrise prayer and meditation

13
epilogue

244 Sorrow, Moving On

Special thanks to those who helped make this project possible:

FRANK MESSINA, PETER PECERE, DR. NANINE HENDERSON, DAWN TILTON & MIKE DRISKELL, Amanda Buck, David Amram, Cameron Crowe & Nancy Wilson, Mark Reese & Patti Brand, Theo Dorgan, Bob Holman, Anonymous, Gui Stuart & Angela Dobbs, Dr. Fred Fischer, Michael & Kris Young, Ian McIlvaine, Helina Berryman, Joshua Thomas, Che Clark, Thayne Clark, Colin & Linda Shaddick, Rob Zoschke, Dean & Susan McClain, J.B. Wilson, Todd Autry, Maria Resee Wilson, Kyle Anne Citrynell, Mark Bacon, Nathanial Whitehead & Jessica Sharpenstein, Heidi & Daniel Freeman, Jeremy Hogan, Elizabeth Jasper, Andy Cook, Dr. John Rocco, Dan & Mary Barth, Dan Roberts, Edwin & Greta Whitehead, Gene Williams, Danny Matherly, Dr. Suzette Henke & Dr. Jim Rooney, Jan & Conny Pankow, Dave Engel, Karen Elize Brumley, Kate Klein, Tommy James, Diana Stuart, Laura Thompson & Crow, Nita Campbell, Tyrone Cotton, Zoe Artemis, Richard Deakin, and Angell Crawford-King.

**for my children, my grandchildren,
and all my children to come**

sometimes necessary to go down
when climbing mountain

failure
has been
my greatest
success

Listening is
the greatest art of all

1
fields of purple morning glories

Sarah Elizabeth & Ron Whitehead, Wedding on Natural Bridge, Kentucky 2003
photo by James Walck

For My Children, Now Grown

for Nathanial, Rani, and Dylan

buried deep in you are the first words you heard
upon entering this world words spoken by me

your father holding you close you and I staring
deep into each other filled with love every

word residing still deep inside you every word
is filled with hope and love and welcome

and thank you for coming for being my friend every
word is filled with unconditional love every

word is still there nestled deep blanketing your
heart providing comfort every word will remain

gifts to sustain to bring joy and adventure words
of encouragement of unconditional love for you

my children I held you in my arms I spoke
with you privately God and angels our only witness

remembering now those words I spoke knowing they
shelter and nurture you I rest easier the anxiety subsides

fields of purple morning glories

for Sarah

fields of purple morning glories
   the love we made last night
outside morning's window purpled bliss
   the love we made this morning
purple morning glories everywhere
   the love we made going home
gloried purple Montgomery morning
   call me I love you
what time is it? purple morning time
   I love you purple
a sandlot of purple morning glories
   outside our morning window
purple morning gloried Montgomery
   purple wounded town
from bluegrass to purple glory we go
   embracing dawn we are one
fields of purple morning glories
   will you marry me?
fields of purple morning glories
   we make love from behind
fields of purple morning glories
   we make love front and behind
fields of purple morning glories
   we make love upside down inside out
fields of purple morning glories
   we love in the round
fields of purple morning glories
   we are a traveling circus
purple gypsies magic moving mystery
   theatre traveling salvation poetry music medicine show
fields of purple morning glories

    we married then and there
fields of purple morning glories
    purple wedding natural bridge
fields of purple morning glories
    all day all night flight
fields of purple morning glories
    life together pure delight
fields of purple morning glories
    from Alabama to Kentucky
fields of purple morning glories
    scattered round the world
fields of purple morning glories
    spread our ashes cross purple
fields of morning glory the love
    we share in fields of
purple morning gloried love
    is all there is

love on a rainy day

for Sarah

fogged windows
wet floorboard

the red '67 Mustang

winds us down
flooding Kentucky

backroads Lincoln
country heart of

the world redbuds
dogwoods blooming

love
on a rainy day

My Beautiful Mutant

for Sarah

ode to joy
my beautiful mutant

walks naked through
morning's door her bath

dark she is head to toes
her long hair shines

brown straight waves
breasts full brown nipples

round bright her eyes
Cherokee brown bright

dark glowing radiant
long limbs toes fingers waist

slender sleek athletic runner
shoulders arms legs sensual

strong hips vibrant vibrate her
smile melts Italian marble

the sun rises lights Kentucky
pink yellow blue morning sky

sunrise ode to joy
my bride my beautiful mutant

To Ballard to the wilderness we go

for Sarah

listen
listen to the song to the song
of the harrier of the brown thrasher
of the yellow-breasted chat of the red-tailed hawk

look
look at the running at the leaping
deer and squirrel
at the slithering rattlesnake cottonmouth
copperhead

look and listen
while wandering sloughs bottomlands
scattered stands of hardwood of bald cypress
look and listen to the soaring bald eagle
to the dove the prothonatary warbler
the yellow-throated warbler
the Mississippi kite listen and look
at the woodlands the lakes
the swamps the rivers
listen and look to where waters rivers meet

dream
dream yourself there
to Ballard we go to the wilderness
lost and forgotten Kentucky beauty
west of west as far as far
nowhere else but here
last stop
to Ballard to the wilderness we go

Dream

for Sarah

if I were a free man, unencumbered,
I'd write a poem describing the dream
I had last night

we were in a graveyard
full moon, meteors,
middle of a clear day
on a hill, summer breeze,
in the country, creek, trees

a church, ancient, catholic,
St. Rose, beauty everywhere,
high summer, wondering
what the future holds

but being not a free man, encumbered,
I can't write a poem describing the dream
I had last night

Your Breath
for Sarah

your breath
spring breeze

washes my face
heals me

at 3am
your eyes

open
look deep

into me
we press

closer
and closer

into each other
we merge

your breath
in my ear

warms
my brain

my mind
now dwells

in my heart
your breath
saves me

Christmas, the old ways, and you

for Sarah

    a Dubl Handi wood and metal washboard, from Edward,
       your Grandpa, he passed away in April
    a long-handled oak pot-stirrer, from Virginia,
       your Grandmother, she turned 86 in December
    a two-pronged hickory pitchfork, handcarved by Daddy Charlie,
       my great-grandfather, gone when I was 13, gift from Mama
    a cast iron woodhandled Bacon Press, with pig and flowers etched,
       from Mama, she turned 74 in May
    a gently smiling Raggedy Ann, handmade for you,
       for your first Christmas, when you were one month old, by Kay,
       your Mom, she turned 56 in March, the doll rediscovered by you,
       in a closet, in your Dad's house, the house you spent
       your first five years in
    a Davy Crockett plate, your Dad ate all his boyhood meals on,
       from Lee, your Dad, he turned 60 in June

fading photographs and letters, scratched phonograph records,
    Native American relics, the old ways claim us

Christmas gifts, in 2006, the old ways, come home to us
Christmas gifts, you, at 27, you are the old ways
Christmas gifts, the old ways, dwell in you, in our warm home
Christmas gifts, the old ways, and you

old veins

sunlight after snow
december 1st morning
age spots surface

on my right arm leaning
twards window light
trees leafless the sparrow

slides down the windshield
of our parked 88 Toyota
222,000 mile pickup truck

the rose the veins the olding
nearly ancient veins green to
white to pink to darkening

light fades snow then rain
returns songs on the radio
books red wine flowers on

the table I sit in my windowed
rocking chair 3rd floor living
these days in a tree house

apartment in a city in the
country considering reviewing
seeing my life past present

future what has been what is
what remains only the wind
knows for sure which way

my life will go Christmas
songs return to the radio
it's December winter approaching

a carved cedar rocking chaired
staff in the corner a cello grinds
gentle romance by the wall

what is life but love
loving veins growing old
blood flowing slowing the

rose on the table leans
twards the song twards the
cello the veins of the rose

freeze mid-stream
rose blood stops the
sun shines snow falls

my rose body dies
my soul sings grace
gratefully travels on

I Strive No More

It is over
the striving
the striving to achieve
the striving is over

I strive no more forever

The time has come
for letting go
letting go all hope of fruition
letting go all and everything

I let go forever

Finally my heart is open
my heart
my heart is filled with tears and laughter
my heart cries and sings

My heart is eternally grateful

I strive no more forever
I let go forever
my heart is eternally grateful

geothermal piano
13 Grandmothers and Sarah do the Sun Dance
with wild horses

for Sarah

your shadow detached itself
and danced with you

wild horse mother and colt
kissed your hands

you turned and saw yourself
holding a baby (ours? I hope) in your arms

beetles made love under
the ancient tree of life

an entire colony of prairie
dogs laughed their asses off

13 Grandmothers smoked peace
pipe   7 teepees on the hill

time vanished

orange west wind sunset lasts
4 hours   bear and eagle

in no time

claws ripped into flesh
and pulled   the wind the wind

no clocks

singing   high pitched singing
soft spiritual lullaby healing

Sarah song for Mother Earth
for all the tribes

watch time disappear

healings potions rubbed vigorously
on back and chest and breasts

no time

visions dances animal spirit
tiger woman leaps bounds

in and out of river eats leaves
from tree   you sleep with

branch from sacred Sun Dance tree
you sing dance you are healed

you found your people
you are home   geothermal

piano must be moved   Sun Dance
magic land life will never

be the same again   the dance
the Sun Dance   you and 13 Grandmothers

welcome home my love welcome
home to your Kentucky tree house lover

there's no time like no time at all

welcome home Sarah
I Love You!!!!!!!!!!!!!!(14)
Ron
june 24, 2007
Kentucky
AHA

2
from Kentucky he came

Ron, age 5, and dog, Ohio County, Kentucky 1956, photo by Greta Whitehead

Old Blue Got Run Over by A Coal Truck on Christmas

Old Blue went everywhere I went. If I rested in the orange sagebrush on the side of old Render hill, back of our farm, up next to the woods, Old Blue rested by my side. We watched the clouds shape shift. When I talked, Old Blue listened. When Old Blue talked, I listened. Through the woods, across the fields, over the creeks, down the dirt and gravel roads, whether I was on foot or horse or bicycle, Old Blue was always with me. Old Blue was a hunting dog, one of the best. But I loved Old Blue cause he was one of the best friends I'd ever had.

One Christmas, when I was 10, Old Blue got run over by a coal truck.

To this day the coal trucks never stop running. They all go too fast. They're always overloaded spilling lumps of coal from here to Kingdom Come. Can't count the times I've dodged flying coal. And they tear our roads up. But nobody ever stops them or slows them down. Nobody ever does anything about them.

Old Blue drug himself into a thicket he called home. I crawled in there with him. Every day for a week I took him water and food. He drank a little water but he refused to eat. He just looked at me with the most pitiful eyes I've ever seen.

I stayed with him the entire week cept when I had to do my chores and at night when it got too cold. I found an old wore out blanket in the utility room and I put that on him to help keep him warm. But even the blanket didn't stop him from shivering.

Old Blue died on the last day of the year, New Year's Eve. Tore me up. Like losing a member of the family.

Growing up on a farm in Kentucky was a gift, a gift beyond measure, beyond words. I had 23 dogs, every one a friend. Every last one of my friends got run over by coal trucks.

The Sound of Falling Snowflakes

1962. I was 12.

One afternoon, late, a little before dark, snow started falling. It snowed all night.

My brother Brad and I slept in the unfinished attic. Through the night I listened to winter's wind whistling through the cracks in our walls, I listened to winter's wind and snow weaving songs accompanied by the cedar and pine trees surrounding and protecting our home.

Before daybreak I heard Mama and Daddy downstairs, Daddy loading the furnace with coal then going out the back door headed to the barn to feed the animals, Mama in the kitchen cooking breakfast. She was singing, quietly, "Amazing Grace." I smelled bacon and biscuits and gravy and coffee. Yes I was already drinking coffee. Started when I was 6.

I woke Brad up. Brad was a sound sleeper. I said "Hey, wake up. Let's go see how much snow we got. Hey, get up. We've got to go milk the cows, chop the ice on the pond, and bring the coal in. Come on, Mama's cooking breakfast. I'm going down."

Brad and I had breakfast with Mama and Daddy. As always Mama's cooking was delicious. We ate every crumb. Brad licked his plate.

Daddy left for work at the mines.

After Brad and I finished our morning chores I got my .410 shotgun and went hunting.

It had snowed over a foot during the night and giant flakes were still falling. The snow wasn't letting up.

I walked and walked and walked. I was in awe of the beauty, all the beauty that surrounded me. I lost track of time.

I found myself in a field surrounded by woods. All round me the wind whispered through the limbs the branches of the barren trees, the wind whispered through the fur of the evergreen trees. A lone crow cawed in the distance, searching its way home.

It was then I realized that I was hearing a sound louder than any other, a loud but gentle and soft sound, the sound of falling snowflakes, the sound of falling snowflakes.

Moxley and Eirene
Moonshine King Burgoo Queen

Mama gave me a tin cup when I was a boy. Til I left home, when I was 17, I wore a thin rope, in place of a belt, to hold my pants up. I've always been skinny. I kept my tin cup, and a knife with a bottle opener, on my rope. They both came in handy many times including, and especially, my last visit with Moxley and Eirene.

I was 16, a year away from leaving home, leaving home for good, leaving home forever. I'd come to visit Moxley and Eirene, travelin by boat, alone. I didn't know how many more times I'd have this opportunity. It was a crisp clear day in early September. The sad and glad of early fall filled me up. It felt good but it ached with loneliness too.

Some of you know that several miles southwest of Centertown, 27 miles from Owensboro, Owensboro, the self-proclaimed burgoo capitol of the world, deep, and I mean deep, in the bottoms where the bobcats still live, on an island on a tight curve of Green River, the deepest river in the world, with catfish that have swallowed children whole, the Green River, with nests of water moccasins in every cove, on a tight curve of the Green River lived, in a wicked, crooked dirt hut old Moxley and his wife Eirene. The island, called Toad's Island, rose, peaking with a small hill, above the Green. It had flooded only once, back in '37. Unlike most of the Irish and Scots in Ohio County, the fifth largest county, and one of the poorest, in Kentucky, home of Bill Monroe, the father of Bluegrass music, resting across the Green River from Muhlenberg County and Paradise, unlike most of the Irish and Scots Moxley's parents had come from Hungary and Eirene's from Greece back in the 1800s.

When I was a boy I visited Moxley and Eirene with Daddy or Grandaddy Dick. We stopped by after runnin trot lines. Some city people might call them trout lines but we never caught no trout on them: we caught catfish, turtles, snakes and eels all of which occasionally found their way into Eirene's burgoo, the best, and most peculiar, unlike any other, burgoo in the world. Eirene was the burgoo queen. Although few will admit it, folks from miles away, including all the way from Owensboro, eventually found their way to Toad's Island, down on the Green River, and borrowed the recipes, which continue to be used on rare, private, and special occasions, for Eirene's burgoo and Moxley's moonshine whiskey. Moxley was the moonshine king.

Moxley and Eirene had an orchard and a garden but Moxley always said he lived on snake, snappin turtle, possum, and moonshine whiskey. By the time I was 16 I'd seen him eatin and drinkin all of them more than once and with his big red and purple nose I figured he was tellin the truth. He kept his moonshine still right in front of their hut. They had a one-eyed black cat with no tail called Spit and a three-legged dog called Tick. Eirene, I guessed, was probably a witch but a decent one and by the time I first met her, when I was a boy, she may have forgotten most of what she once knew.

But she had remembered how to make burgoo, the most unusual and distinctively flavored burgoo I've ever tasted. Same was true of Moxley's moonshine. I can barely even approximate their magic recipes. I was a poor witness especially once Moxley began offerin pourin his moonshine, God's Tears, into my tin cup. It was the smoothest hard liquor I've ever, in my entire life, tasted. My vision blurred as I watched Moxley on my left and Eirene on my right. Sometimes they became one, not too pretty, person. But, despite their strangeness, I always liked both of them so no matter how ugly they looked as one person it didn't matter, I didn't care, I just sat there watchin and grinnin and smellin while they brewed the burgoo and the moonshine.

Moxley poured in spring water which he collected runnin directly out of the side of their Toad's Island hill. He added pure cane sugar, cracked corn and malt. He always cut the first gallon with water cause it was so strong. It kicked harder than a mule or an udder sore milk cow. Sometimes he added burnt sugar and water to change the colorin. He did that for variety. While Moxley was cookin up his strange brew my attention wandered back and forth so I watched Eirene cook her burgoo too. I watched her make burgoo several times, over the years, and it was always different dependin on what she had available. This particular time, the last time I saw her make it, when I was 16, she killed a chicken, snuck up behind it and cut its head off before it knew what happened, then she plucked it and tossed it in, then instead of beef or pork, she added chunks of snappin turtle, possum, water moccasin, and eel. Even though fish isn't common to burgoo I'm pretty sure, despite the moonshine I'd drunk, that she threw in several pieces of catfish. I'd brought her two rabbits I killed huntin with Daddy. I helped her skin them then she threw them in, bones and all, didn't even cut off the heads. Of course the pot, which was on an open fire in front of the hut, was filled with water from the river. She also mixed in some dirty dish water. For some reason I never discovered, before addin the water she first placed river rocks in the bottom of the pot. Once the water was ready she tossed in tomatoes, potatoes, onions, garlic, cabbage, peppers, carrots, corn, beans, peas, ketchup, salt, pepper, thyme, vinegar, sauces, homemade red wine, plenty of Moxley's moonshine, pinches of a variety of herbs, then she said words I didn't understand, maybe Greek, the language of her ancestors, and she said them like she was castin a spell. It was spooky the way she chanted those words gettin a glazed faraway look in her dark eyes. Good Lord I knew it was gonna be good. It always was. She cooked it for hours. I'm not sure how many hours cause I passed out.

When I woke up the sun had set. It was a beautiful starry night. The full moon was risin. A pack of wild dogs was barkin way off in the distance, up river. Crickets, katydids, frogs, and lightnin bugs brightened the night providin a brilliant sound and light show. Eirene and Moxley handed me food and drink, burgoo and moonshine, best food in the world, bar none. We stayed up late, into the night, sharin stories, listenin close to each other, to the bobcat's mournful wail, listenin to the spirits walkin the earth late, late at night when the vail tween worlds disappears.

The next mornin, just after daybreak, a buzzin fly woke me up. All three of us had fallen asleep on the ground, up close to the fire which had fallen to a dull ember, almost out. The sun was crackin the sky over the trees east of the Green. I rose, walked silently to my boat and glided away. It was my final visit, the last time I saw my dear ancient friends Moxley and Eirene, moonshine king burgoo queen.

Searching For Abraham Lincoln

        visited Springfield
        flew to Louisville
        drove Bardstown Road to
           St. Catharine College
           then on to The Starving Artist Café

   Welcome to Springfield, Kentucky

      wandered   Main street   side streets
               lost   for hours
          small suitcase weighed down with
        heavy words
             The Emancipation Proclamation
             The Gettysburg Address
          Abraham Lincoln's words his works his life
            biography of his boyhood
          he was spiritual intuitive psychic

"That on the 1st day of January, A.D. 1863, all persons held as slaves…
   shall be then, thenceforward, and forever free…"

            and I'm searching for Abraham Lincoln
          on Bardstown Road   Beech Fork   Lincoln Homestead

"Four score and seven years ago, our fathers brought forth upon this
   continent a new nation: conceived in liberty, and dedicated to the
   proposition that all men are created equal."

   Welcome to Springfield, Kentucky   Abraham Lincoln country

          I walked Kentucky   into the wind
           dark and bloody ground
           jewel in the lotus

omphalos
heart of the world
holy triangle
sacred
Abbey of Gethsemani   St. Catharine's   St. Joseph's
Trappist monks   Dominican nuns
coal mined   bituminous gold   nearly gone
smokestacks   power plants   largest shovel in the world
profane
Native Americans   pioneers   farmers   coal miners
strong women
poets   writers   musicians

in Kentucky music is mountainous

and I'm searching for Abraham Lincoln
the greatest President of them all
he saved us from ourselves

and here I am in Springfield
heart of Kentucky
Lincoln country

who will save us now

and I'm searching for Abraham Lincoln
maybe Edgar Cayce can help
modern day prophet
one of the great psychics of all time
and from Hopkinsville, Kentucky

maybe Muhammad Ali   "The Greatest"   from Louisville
maybe Muhammad Ali can point the way
with his International Peace Center

26

"float like a butterfly
sting like a bee"

oh Muhammad oh Muhammad
will you please help me cause

I'm searching for Abraham Lincoln

and the rivers and creeks of Kentucky
Ohio, Kentucky, Mississippi, Barren, Big Sandy,
Rough, Elkhorn, Green
spray us with tears
of Mexican immigrants
who for forty days and forty nights have stood
in the fields outside America's door
knocking   denied entry   denied
Churchill Downs   The Derby   singing
"My Old Kentucky Home"   knocking
on our doors   pleading   "let us come in"
"let us live in your beautiful Kentucky Home"

and I'm searching for Abraham Lincoln

walking up hills   mountains   The Knobs   The Appalachians
Natural Bridge
bowing to gravity
leaning backward with my long hair sweeping the path
as I descend the wind and the descent flatten me
and now my muscles are green and yellow and red pain
sustaining my search
drink red wine and strong coffee
at The Starving Artist Café

and I'm searching for Abraham Lincoln

I want love to have its way

I want us to stand united   not divided
One world One people   together   in peace and harmony

and searching for Abraham Lincoln
I crawl through Kentucky
so many diamonds I find   birthed from the deep dark mines
Iroquois Cherokee Shawnee Tribes   Daniel Boone   Henry Clay
Abraham Lincoln
Elizabeth Madox Roberts   James Still   Bill Monroe
Loretta Lynn   Muhammad Ali   Hunter S. Thompson
Johnny Depp   Scott & Aimee Mullins
Harry Dean Stanton   Ned Beatty   Adolf Rupp
Rick Pitino   Lionel Hampton   Wendell Berry
John Jacob Niles   Pee Wee Reese   The Everly Brothers
Merle Travis   Rosemary Clooney   Edgar Cayce
Robert Penn Warren   Thomas Merton
the literary renaissance
Appalshop   Bluegrass   Bourbon   Beautiful Women
in Kentucky   the moon shines   comets are loud
My Old Kentucky Home   Churchill Downs   Louisville Slugger
The Great Outhouse Blowout   Penn's Store   Gravel Switch
Kentucky Fried Chicken   Wildcats   Cardinals

and as I search for Abraham Lincoln
I sit in The Starving Artist Café
on a rainy October day
drinking red wine

why do men still drink wine
and women still water

beautiful paintings cover the walls
and yes when I give readings round the world
I hear 3rd world voices monks and nuns
Ernesto Cardenal   Nicanor Parra
Daniel Berrigan   Thomas Merton

                    Mother Teresa
                        The Dalai Lama
            pierce the world's terrors chanting singing praying
                                            for love
                                            for peace

                and I'm searching for Abraham Lincoln
                "the one who'll shake the ones unshaken
                    the fearless one"

                and searching for Abraham Lincoln
                    in the St. Catharine College Library
        I look in Lawrence Ferlinghetti's   yes San Francisco Ferlinghetti
who stood
                at Merton's grave with me
        I look in Ferlinghetti's A Coney Island of the Mind and
                                Pictures of the Gone World
                and I read

            "Christ climbed down
            from His bare tree
            this year
            and softly stole away into
            some anonymous Mary's womb again
        where in the darkest night
            of everybody's anonymous soul
            He awaits again
            an unimaginable
            and impossibly
            Immaculate Reconception
            the very craziest
            of Second Comings."

                    and I'm standing in The Starving Artist Café
                        on Main Street in Springfield, Kentucky
                                    the heart of Kentucky

                                29

                    the heart of the world
          on this rainy October Tuesday
          and the wind and the rain whisper
     welcome   welcome   welcome
                         to Springfield

and I'm searching searching searching for Abe Honest Abe
               searching for Abraham Lincoln
          in Springield
                    welcome to Springfield, Kentucky USA

The Dance
a choral, orchestral, song poem

for Christopher Seal and Sarah Elizabeth

silent dance…holy dance…winds cross…ancestral waters…

we wear these garments…dwell in these temples…

briefly…we are…short lived…temporary…

sun worshippers…silent dance…the drum speaks…

instinct…the drum…earth heart…beats pure…

we…are delicate pale pink blossoms…on…

Van Gogh's almond tree…our fine attire covering bones…

the bones of life…loving bones…bones in love…

silent dance…rhythm…balance…

names carved…on trees…on rocks…

names handwritten…in bibles…aging ageless memories…

love never fades…winds cross ancestral rivers…

silent dance…the dance…a waltz…

fragrant…spring wind carries us to the end…

of…the night…listen listen listen…

down in the valley…the valley so low…

hang your head over…hear the wind blow…

hear the wind blow dear…hear the wind blow…

hang your head over…hear the wind blow…

I hear Mama calling…calling from far away…

throw your arms round me…before it's too late…

throw your arms round me…feel my heart break…

I hear Mama calling…calling from far away…

feel my heart break love…feel my heart break…

throw your arms round me…feel my heart break…

I hear Mama calling…calling from far away…

down in the valley…the valley so low…

hang your head over…hear the wind blow…

hear the wind blow dear…hear the wind blow…

hang your head over…hear the wind blow…

silent dance…holy dance…winds cross…ancestral waters…

we wear these garments…dwell in these temples…

briefly…we are…short lived…temporary…

sun worshippers…silent dance…the drum speaks…

instinct…the drum…earth heart…beats pure…

we…are delicate pale pink blossoms…on…

Van Gogh's almond tree…our fine attire covering bones…

the bones of life…loving bones…bones in love…

silent dance…rhythm…balance…

names carved…on trees…on rocks…

names handwritten…in bibles…aging ageless memories…

love never fades…winds cross ancestral rivers…

silent dance…the dance…a waltz…

fragrant…spring wind carries us to the end…

of…the night…listen listen listen…

I hear Mama calling…calling from far away…

I hear the winds sighing…through every bush and tree…

where my dear Mama's sleeping…away from…

so far away from me…tears from my eyes are flowing…

deep sorrow shades my brow…cold in her grave…

she's sleeping…I hear Mama calling…calling from far away…

but I have no Mama now…I hear Mama calling…

but I have no Mama now…I see the pale moon shining…

on Mama's white tomb stone…the rose bush round them twining…

the tomb and rose are just like Mama…all alone…

just like me a-weeping…cold dewdrops shade my brow…

cold in her grave she's sleeping…I hear Mama calling…

calling from far away…but I have no Mama now…

my life is ever lonely…my heart is troubled sore…

her dearest presence only…can make me weep no more…

she's gone from me to heaven…deep sorrow shades my brow…

the sacred tie is broken…I hear my Mama calling…

but I have no Mama now…I have no Mama now…

sad was the hour of parting…she spoke in words so sweet…

my child my child I'm dying…we must in heaven meet…

oh yes I'll meet you Mama…on that eternal shore…

and we will live forever…where parting is no more…

I hear Mama calling…calling from far away…

listen listen listen…down in the valley below…

down in the valley…the valley so low…

silent dance…holy dance…winds cross…ancestral waters…

we wear these garments…dwell in these temples…

briefly…we are…short lived…temporary…

sun worshippers…listen listen listen…

down in the valley…the valley so low…

silent dance…the drum speaks…

instinct…the drum…earth heart…beats pure…

we…are delicate pale pink blossoms…on…

Van Gogh's almond tree…our fine attire covering bones…

the bones of life…loving bones…bones in love…

listen listen listen…down in the valley…the valley so low…

silent dance…rhythm…balance…

names carved…on trees…on rocks…

names handwritten…in bibles…aging ageless memories…

love never fades…winds cross ancestral waters…

I hear Mama calling…calling from far away…

silent dance…the dance…a waltz…

fragrant...spring wind carries us to the end...

of...the night...listen listen listen...

hear Mama calling...calling from far away...

from down in the valley...the valley so low...

I hear Mama calling...calling me home...

listen listen listen...the dance...the dance...the dance...

Ron Whitehead
September 12, 2006
Kentucky
AHA

"The Dance" includes Sarah Elizabeth's "Silent Dance," Ron Whitehead's "The Dance," and the traditional songs "Down In The Valley" and "No Mother Now." All works rearranged, changed, reworked, quilted into "The Dance," a long poem, by Ron Whitehead, written for Christopher Seal to be incorporated into his musical composition for voice, Sarah Elizabeth, and orchestra.

lost poem: intimations

for Sarah

1.

the child, beyond reason,
is wise. and i wish
my days spent bounding,
a child, in nature.

2.

there was a time when the yard, the garden, the orchard, the barn,
the pond,
the meadow, the chicken coop, the fields,
the cows, the horses, the pigs, the dogs, the cats,
the woods, the hills, the valleys, the streams, the creeks, the rivers,
the paths, the dirt roads, the gravel roads,
all of nature,
untrammeled and barely trammeled,
earth and sky
shone in heavenly light.
every day, every night,
sunrise, sunset,
sun, moon, and stars,
rain, sleet, hail, snow,
wind and calm,
cloudy and clear,
warm and cold,
spring, summer, fall, winter,
trees, leaves, flowers, grass,
planting, hoeing, harvesting,
birth, the journey, death,
all of nature,
all and everything
shone in heavenly light.

3.
a child, beyond reason,
is wise. i let go all longing.
i wish no more. i walk out the door.
i will spend my remaining days bounding,
a child, in nature.

3
driving 110milesperhour on Bardstown Road with Allen Ginsberg

Allen Ginsberg & Ron Whitehead, Kentucky 1992 photo by Charlie Coddington

On First Reading Jack Kerouac's
ON THE ROAD

Down and Out in Kentucky

Part VII

For Madmen Only

We'd just finished our second fifth of Southern Comfort
and the mescaline was kickin in
Jimi Hendrix crosses borders threatening to ascend towards heaven
with lightning and thunder he plays
Dylan's "All Along The Watchtower" stereo loud as it will go
here in the only underground bookstore in Kentucky
For Madmen Only
shelves and bins stocked with books and records from
City Lights and bookpeople   San Francisco
Atlantis and Alligator   New Orleans
teas and herbs   candles and incense   from mountain communes
turquoise blue Spiritual Sky
and next door in
The Store
our head shop
paraphernalia   water beds   posters   GROW YOUR OWN
blankets and clothes from India   Native American jewelry
and we're serving the new consciousness
inspired by the one and only King of The Dharma Bums
         Jack Kerouac
and yes there's Lawrence Ferlinghetti
    Gary Snyder   Richard Brautigan   Ken Kesey
Allen Ginsberg   William Carlos Williams   William Blake
Hermann Hesse   Knut Hamsun   Dostoevski   Nietzsche
Bukowski   Thomas Merton   The Dalai Lama   Gandhi
Burroughs   LeRoi Jones   Diane di Prima

Hunter S. Thompson
and more more more
with Robert Johnson   Hound Dog Taylor   Howlin' Wolf
Jimi Hendrix   Patti Smith
and always Bob Dylan   Bob Dylan   Bob Dylan
on the stereo
but we're Down and Out in Kentucky
failin like no others dare fail
and we're always on the outside   outsiders   outlaws
bein told you don't fit you ain't shit what the fuck you doin here
and so On The Road
is where we live   travelin   travelin   travelin
in search of   IT
headed out of Kentucky cross the usa coast to coast
down to Mexico determined to
keep on keeping on truckin til the wheels fall off and burn
just passin thru searchin searchin yes after all these years
still searchin for IT and yet somewhere somehow one day one moment
at the heights of Machu Picchu we went further in traveled deeper
on the inner road   we entered the third kingdom the fourth dimension
where lies the synthesis of apparently irreconcilable differences
and in the heart of The Big Bang Epiphany we discovered
that the power and the glory of IT is bound in the grace
of forgiveness   of Beating Karma through love compassion
of persevering through desperate circumstances so now
we GO GO GO   we Never Give Up   recognizing Now that
The Road   that Jack Kerouac's Road   that our Road
always leads On.

Kerouac's Daughter

Over the grave you stand gentle
smile   arms outstretched   open

hands welcoming   Christ there
in the tomb at least his old bones

not rotting rather becoming white
light white heat like his writing

holy spirit Jack Kerouac your lost
father holy ghost wandering now

in other realms like he did on earth
he does in heaven his books and

yours published there where you
in darkest night in darkest night

comes wind weaves night violin
wolf song comes wind weaves

night violin wolf song in darkest
night in darkest night where you

steal away where you steal away
into everybody's anonymous soul

Kerouac's compassionate daughter
poet birthing the global literary

community "an unimaginable and
impossibly immaculate Reconception

the very craziest of Second Comings"

Without Blinking: Zen & the Art of Driving 100milesperhour past Mayor Abramson & others from Twice Told Coffeehouse on Bardstown Road to the Airport

Part IV: Down & Out in Kentucky

Allen Ginsberg: The Bridge

It's not legal today to drive 100milesperhour up or down Bardstown Road and it wasn't legal midday October 2nd 1992 but I had a feeling ever since early morning when I picked Allen Ginsberg up at The Seelbach preparing to spend at least half a day roaming the backstreets alleys and riverfront of Louisville searching for Walt Whitman's ghost plus hopefully a pair of khakis from Goodwill on Broadway for Allen since he'd somehow ripped the pair he had on his only pair at the University of Louisville reading the night before reading and singing to an audience of 1,500 which was awed Ahed and often teareyed electrified or maybe he ripped them at The Bristol round 2AM anyway while waiting inside the door of Allen's room ready to exit carrying his bags he said "just a minute" and took a leak and I, feeling a little uncomfortable, asked "what time does your flight leave" and for some reason I wasn't satisfied with his answer so after lunch at Twice Told Coffeehouse after we looked in at Guitar Emporium for a lefthanded banjo for Peter Orlovsky but no one waited on us so Allen left his card we stepped back onto the street into the borrowed car with Kent and Mark climbing into back seats I prodded again "why don't you just double check your airline ticket" and he did and yes his flight is an hour earlier than he'd remembered and we have less than ten minutes to departure and he has to be in Lowell Massachusetts tonight cause he's the featured poet at the Annual Jack Kerouac Festival so I'm driving like a bat out of hell 100milesperhour midday Bardstown Road my senses open employing maximum peripheral awareness watching for pedestrians cars cops surrounding our borrowed car and us with lightning electric white light white heat as we speed to airport passing Mayor Abramson in limo and others all open mouthed gaping staring in disbelief and I tell Allen that we're bringing Amiri Baraka in two weeks and Allen's excited talking as fast as I'm driving telling all about Amiri and I look in rearview mirror and see Kent and Mark mouths open wondering whether we'll survive without getting arrested or killed or killing on this yet another insane trip and finally we arrive at airport I hit the flashers and we're off walking as fast as we can knowing Allen's health not great we jump on moving walkway still walking fast when suddenly Allen takes off running and Kent Mark and I look at each other scratch our heads and by time Allen ten yards ahead we leap into run and when we're within three yards he turns stops and just as we are midstride airborn mouths ajar feeling like 3 stooges 3 monkeys 3 idiots Allen takes photo then turns in stride and we're all off running again arriving as gate being pulled to we yell "WAIT" then Allen turns gives us each hug kiss on cheek says sincerest "Thank You" and is gone.

Calling the Toads

Part I: The Antinomian Fire This Time

A threshold has been crossed with the passing of Allen Ginsberg. He had become he is (as millions round the world celebrate his passing) a symbolic figure representing personal freedoms which today are under attack by new age cult fascist Cromwellian Roundhead Puritan Christian Coalition religion government led by Rush Limbo Newt Gingrich Pat Buchanan Jesse Helms Jerry Falwell Pat Robertson Ralph Reed and others much as personal freedoms were under attack in the 50s by Joseph McCarthy Richard Nixon J. Edgar Hoover and others in that decade when The Beat Generation achieved notoriety through the publication of such acclaimed (and censored) works as HOWL (1956) by Allen Ginsberg, ON THE ROAD (1957) by Jack Kerouac, A CONEY ISLAND OF THE MIND (1958) by Lawrence Ferlinghetti, and NAKED LUNCH (1959) by William S. Burroughs. The difference is that, with advancements in technology, governments, militaries, and corporations now pose an ever greater threat to personal (and, by extension, community) freedoms.

Today "Specialization" is sold on every corner, fed in every home, brainwashed in to every student, every young person. We are told that the only way to succeed, here at the end of the 20th Century, and certainly tomorrow in the 21st Century, is to put all our time, energy, learning and focus into one area, one field, one specialty (math, science, computer technology, business). If we don't we will fail. We are subtly and forcefully, implicitly and explicitly, encouraged to deny the rest of who we are, our total self, selves, our holistic being. The postmodern brave new world seems to reside inside the computer via The Web with only faint peripheral recognition of the person, the individual (and by extension the real global community), the real human being operating the machine. The idea of and belief in specialization as the only path, only possibility, has sped up the fragmentation, the alienation which began to grow rapidly within the individual, radically reshaping culture, a century ago with the birth of those Machiavellian revolutions in technology, industry, and war. And with the growing fracturing fragmentation and alienation comes the path - anger, fear, anxiety, angst, ennui, nihilism, depression, despair - that, for the person of action, leads to suicide. Unless, through our paradoxical leap of creative faith we engage ourselves in the belief, which can become a life mission, that regardless of the consequences, we can, through our engagement, our actions, our loving life work, make the world a better, safer, friendlier place in which to live. Sound naive? What does this have to do with Allen Ginsberg? With Voices Without Restraint? With The Beat Generation? With the so-called and sadly mislabeled Generation X? With The Youth of Today? What place does the Antinomian Voice The Voice of Dissent (in legal terminology an antinomy signifies a contradiction which, for example, in Walt Whitman's historical moment was the condition of slavery in a supposedly free society), the Voice of The Poet, The Voice of The Beat Generation, Allen Ginsberg's Voice, The Voice that (descending/ascending from William Blake, Walt Whitman, Ezra Pound, Henry Miller, & others to Allen Ginsberg), though trembling, speaks out against The Powers That BE, what place does this Outsider Voice have in the real violent world in which we are immersed? Are we too desensitized to the violence, to the fact that in this Century alone we have murdered over 160 million people in one war after another, to even think it worthwhile to consider the possibility of a less violent world? Are we too small, too insignificant to make any kind of difference? The power-mongers have control. What difference can one measly little individual like you or me possibly make, possibly matter?

Today the X and microserf generations are swollen with thousands of young people yearning to express the creative energies buried yet burning like brushfires in their hearts, the smoke seeping from every pore of their beings. They ache to change to heal the world. Is it still possible? Is it too late? Is there anyone (a group?) left to show the way? To set an example? To be a guide? A mentor? James Joyce, King of Modernism, said the idea of the hero was nothing but a damn lie that the primary motivating forces are passion and compassion. As late as 1984 people were laughing at George Orwell. Today, as we finally move into an Orwellian culture of simulation life on the screen landscape, can we remember passion and compassion or has the postmodern ironic satiric deathinlife game laugh killed both sperm and egg? Is there anywhere worth going from here? Is it any wonder that today's youth have adopted Jack Kerouac, Allen Ginsberg, William S. Burroughs, Herbert Huncke, Gregory Corso, Neal Cassady, Lawrence Ferlinghetti, Gary Snyder, David Amram, Amiri Baraka, Robert Creeley, Diane di Prima, Ed Sanders, Anne Waldman, and all other Beat Generation and related poets, writers, artists, musicians as their inspirational, life-affirming ancestors? These are the people who have stood and still stand up against unreasoning power/right/might, looked that power in the eyes and said NO I don't agree with you and this is why. And they have spoken these words, not for money or for fame, but out of life's deepest convictions, out of the belief that we, each one of us - no matter our skin color our economic status our political religious sexual preferences - all of us have the right to live to dream as we choose rather than as some supposed higher moral authority prescribes for us.

Allen Ginsberg and The Beats, who in the next decade will come to be recognized as the most important group of writers and poets in the history of America, have given birth to new generations to new energies which are awakening to the realization that the creative imagination provides salvation from suicide, from death in life, by revealing that there are alternative paths to follow in this world that lead away from the mundane, the superficial into the inspired brilliant fire called life.

Allen Ginsberg and I didn't always get along. In June '95 at New York University's Jack Kerouac Symposium the Anti-Beats demonstrated outside the Loeb Student Center and at the Town Hall reading which featured Ginsberg, Lawrence Ferlinghetti, Gregory Corso, David Amram, Anne Waldman, Lee Ranaldo, and a host of others. The Anti-Beats held banners which read "Rollo Whitehead is the Quintessential Beat" as they marched and chanted "We Want Rollo" and "Rollo Whitehead Save Us From Sellouts." They declaimed disdaining Allen

Ginsberg for selling his letters, and numerous other items he'd collected over decades, to Stanford University for over one million dollars and for appearing in GAP commercials and for earning six figures for his Collected Poems. They claimed that Ginsberg had Sold Out his bohemian anti-establishment peers betraying values he'd preached since his youth. The Press was having a field day.

I walked into Ginsberg's apartment and was given icy stares by Allen, Bob Rosenthal, Peter Hale, Bill Morgan, and Gordon Ball (his General, Lieutenant, Bibliographer, & Editor) all of whom had always been friendly and helpful. "What?" I said. "What did I do now?" "Are you the one leading this Anti-Beat campaign?" they queried back. "Hell No!" and it took me an hour to get to the bottom of the story and convince them I had nothing to do with it which, although I knew many of the Anti-Beats from readings events and publications and had heard a few of them explain the derivation of Rollo Whitehead as Quintessential Beat, I really wasn't involved in their movement. Plus Allen, as an advisor to the literary renaissance and to me, praised my INSOMNIACATHON successes but gave me hell about my financial losses from a 48-hour non-stop music and poetry INSOMNIACATHON which NYU asked me to produce to kickoff their 50-year celebration of The Beat Generation in May of '94. He told me more than once "don't bite off more than you can chew" which believe me I've done more than once in attempts to achieve illumination plus hoping to uplift and inspire others yes well yes I've traveled Interstate Excess till the wheels fell off and burned and well I laughed and I cried when Allen Ginsberg said "you don't want to give poetry a bad name" and I stared back at him in disbelief instantaneously recalling that half of the people I'd ever talked with when Ginsberg's name was mentioned muttered under their breath loathsome vile hatefilled words and the other half sang songs of praise lavishing adoration on this angelheaded rulebreaking boundaryshattering hipster and so what paradoxical advice was this that Allen Ginsberg was giving me?

Allen Ginsberg was a human being more human than most. He said "there's not enough candor not enough honesty in the world, be candid." He was honest about himself about his own life to the point of making some people sick to death of hearing bout the personal details. Many more were offended by his graphic homoerotic love poems. In fact his reading of "Sphincter," which was the first poem he read after intermission at the University of Louisville reading, was the beginning of attacks on me by U of L administration attacks which accelerated after the Amiri Baraka reading attacks which didn't end until Lawrence Ferlinghetti convinced me to divorce myself from university and go independent and out of which was born the global literary renaissance. But just as I saw the fear poet Allen Ginsberg instilled in some I saw liberation in the eyes of others. The fact that this singular lone singing voiced poet had the audacity to stand up in front of God, America, and the President of the University of Louisville and be completely honest be forceful passionate and gentle compassionate without hurting anyone stunned excited set free hundreds thousands in Louisville in America around the world inspiring them to come out of whatever closet they were hiding in and be themselves yet while being themselves always remembering the Beat willingness to believe to believe in life even if that belief couldn't be expressed in conventional terms in a status quo lifestyle and to always remember that Beatitude and Beatific are as much a part of being Beat as anything is.

What did I learn from what do I remember from Allen Ginsberg? What gifts did he share with me? That he loved Bob Dylan but would never be able to consummate that dream cause Dylan is heterosexual. He said Dylan will be remembered longer than the Beats because Dylan is poet bard singing brother of Homer who digs deeper into heart via music. I remember arriving New York City East Village with my family after sunrise allnight drive waiting in van outside his apartment being awakened by street gangs in turfwar standoff with clubs knives guns police arrive twenty minutes after gangs split but police not there for gangs they arrive to escort homeless man from school found sleeping under bleachers in gymnasium. I remember Diane di Prima showing up on street in front of Allen's apartment another visit same time family and I arrived she come to visit for several days. I remember having to front Gregory Corso $100 I didn't really have, Allen's apartment, street methadone so we could travel on to Lowell Massachusetts to read at Kerouac Festival & what Corso spent the $100 on. Allen introduced me to Corso and Herbert Huncke and William S. Burroughs and John Wieners and Robert Creeley and Yevgeny Yevteshenko and Anne Waldman and Ed Sanders and many others and I remember photos of Whitman on kitchen and bedroom walls and Ginsberg getting sick while my daughter Rani and I helped him get what he needed to feel better and I remember meditating at Kerouac's grave after breaking up a fight in a bar between Corso and a stranger and I remember readings and visits in Louisville and Lowell and New York City and Washington D.C. and I remember phone calls and letters and being honored to publish his work and I remember his cathartic candorfilled healing poetry and I honor Allen Ginsberg his life his work and I cherish most of all his giving and I accept it into myself and I intentionally choose to make it one of my ideals one of my spiritual values. to give.

ASHEVILLE
for Allen Ginsberg

right now I'm in Asheville Ashville Ashville
ash yes the right place the right time Ashes
Burned Burned Failed Destroyed Ashes
so what do I do? quit? give up? become cinder for that

longdistanceneverendingrailroadtracktonowhere?

give up? Allen Ginsberg preaches "take a hand" "share the word"
the poetry gospel coming from the gonads the solar plexus
the heart and the head yes thank you Allen for the
energy for the love and my head rises a little
to watch my son, Dylan, and my daughter, Rani Bri,
dancing to the B52s' LOVE SHACK playing on the jukebox
in Asheville and I'm lookin at the moon over the mountain
thinkin bout the kid from Denver and the others from Cheyenne
and I think of Denver and of Dean Moriarty
of Neal Cassady's flame gone gone gone
his naked body lying beside those

longdistanceneverendingrailroadtrackstonowhere

and I hope those kids from the west
hell I hope all of us
keep the funk
keep that Fuck You flame that gnostical turpitude flame
alive
don't let the system break you don't let life break you
so that when the time comes when your time is up
you either go screamin or go with peace in your heart
into that dark night
and now somebody's playing the blues on the piano
and yeah two days ago Rani and I were sittin

at Ginsberg's table in New York City talkin bout Asheville
talkin bout the 20 grand Kent and I lost puttin on that
48-hour non-stop music and poetry INSOMNIACATHON to
kickoff NYU's 50 Year Celebration of The Beat Generation
and I'm talkin with Allen Ginsberg and Herbert Huncke and
Gregory Corso but like when Marc Smith proclaims his name
the audience responds "so what"
and I'm thinkin bout Marc Smith and Spoken Word
and Poetry Alive
and I know few know how much work the workers do the poets do for
poetry
but I know now that the reward the pay is in the experience
and suddenly I remember that the Ash
in Celtic and Scandinavian Mythology is the tree
most generally associated with magic
and yes here I am in Asheville with
all these poets who somehow know the alchemical magical
power of poetry of the word yes manger du livre
eat the book and the word will set you free
and I'm in Asheville thinkin bout Allen Ginsberg
and what he said bout takin somebody's hand
cause we're all in this together we're pullin
we ain't pushin we're lettin it be
we ain't forcin it and I realize that a poem like a
painting or a song is only the representation of
an actual experience the real poem is the event itself
and right now I'm thinkin bout the births of my
three children and each time an angelic face with
Buddah smile appears and I'm thinkin bout Allen Ginsberg
in Asheville and out of the ash that I am I feel an energy
risin through me growin strong comin from poets of
all ages and I'm in Asheville
but it don't feel like failure no more it feels
friendly it feels good it feels strong like some kind of
rebirth
into poetry

into life
it feels like
Resurrection
Right Now
Right Here
in Asheville

Deep Appreciation

by Bob Holman

Dear Ron,

A note of deep appreciation emerges from the bell
Clapper, the diver's helmet bubbling a great gasp
It is freedom in another land, any other terrain, the sea,
Say, or the veldt tundra desert cobbled together like streets
Gathering force to emerge into the central square, Goes.

Amigo, you put your poetry where the body is
And let dance skeletal fragments of possibility
Whose smoke drifts over the dykes, a soft pause
With pure intent and a blessing on a slice of thick
Brown bread. I can't remember when, but I can

Imagine. The world retraces evolution, the fish ponder
And the whole green algaeful glories of existence fin
A book as the bucket turns over on the world. To return
The favor is to mesh the go with the go on   Look you
In the eye and trade gill flutters. Write the poem.

And so now home Kentucky, New York, a kindly ink
Pen of nomenclature to suggest a new society – ah,
The souls of worms, and a late-nite dance craze. The life
Of the mind won't let up – because you's why! Now we're
The bubbles, disappearing into air nouveau. What a trip

To rip the mask from skull and wail into the tooth of crime.
I wouldn't-a missed it for a laugh a second – all the plates
Rattle, and there's nothing left but juggling gravity and death.
That's ok too – long as I'm with you. Friendship as fall settles,
And winter's thought stokes the spring. Brilliant brilliant. All all.
--Bob

Harold Maier Is a Hero of Mine

Harold Maier is a hero of mine
Twice Told Books Twice Told Coffee House

Bardstown Road The Highlands
Harold Maier is a hero of mine

Harold said he opened the
coffee house so I'd have a place

to produce events and we did
the first 2 Insomniacathons

were held at Twice Told
hundreds were turned away

hundreds were turned on
inspired to create many

other Insomniacathons
were held at Twice Told

and other venues round
Louisville plus numerous

other events and always
always Harold was there

and even after Kent went
to Alaska and I went to

Iceland and on and on
our separate ways but

still carrying on The Work
I always found my way back to

Twice Told and Harold was
always there always

with a kind word and
gentle support yes I know

he could be harsh like
Gregory Corso or

Hunter S. Thompson
so can I but with

me and many others he
always offered encouragement

and me being used to
the kick in the teeth

well I'll always more than
anything remember his

kindness Harold Maier
is a hero of mine

From Hank Williams' Grave to Insomniacathon 2003

Keeping The Flame Alive

one week ago Michael Pollock, Andy Cook, Sarah Elizabeth and I
The Viking Hillbilly Apocalypse Revue
drove to Montgomery, Alabama to Foster Dickson's home
on the edge of the historic district and the ghetto
after midnight   drinking red wine on the balcony
gunshots   bam bam bam   a block away   drive by
drug deals gone bad shouts tires squealing more gunshots
bam bam bam
silence   tires squealing
screams
after midnight in Montgomery
a wounded town   long deep scars   open wounds
the city groans moans with old deep pain
and I hear tears streaming rivers down the
bodies of slaves   we ain't done with slavery yet
I don't care what anybody says
despite the 1963 "I Have A Dream"
thank you Martin Luther King Jr speech
and subsequent long overdue civil rights legislation
we ain't done with slavery yet
go to Montgomery, Alabama
go to Powderly, Kentucky
visit the International KKK headquarters
go to Washington D.C.
visit the U.S. Congress
visit the White House
we ain't done with slavery yet
and the next morning in Montgomery, Alabama
red sunrise pink clouds cracking
brand new turquoise sky green earth new day
fresh opportunities

possibilities for change new morning a meadow full of
purple morning glories right outside our window
we reach touch them gently
transported in a pink Cadillac
at sunrise of this new Montgomery, Alabama day
we meditate on Hank Williams' grave
I left a gift
a free INSOMNIACATHON ticket
on his tombstone
I chanted an invitation to
Hank Williams
Time was   Time is   Time will be no more
Please come to
INSOMNIACATHON 2003 please come
to the ending of time
and as I chanted   the wind moved the trees
they began to dance to sway
to the   rhythmic sound of   chanting   to
Time was   Time is   Time will be no more
Please come to INSOMNIACATHON 2003
and suddenly I felt a presence presences
as I chanted thanks thanks to Andy Cook
thanks to Michael Pollock   Sarah Elizabeth
James Walck   Marisa Barnes   Yoruba Mason
Justin Davis   David Amram   Frank Messina
Ken Pyle   The Rudyard Kipling
to all the bands musicians songwriters
to all the poets writers to everyone in
The Global Literary Renaissance
and as I chanted thanks
as Kundalini energy moved through my body
I was lifted up   lifted up   up above
Hank Williams' grave   up above the green red and
yellow blowing autumn leaves
up above the wounded city of Montgomery, Alabama
and surrounded by presences

I recognize now as Hank Williams
Martin Luther King Jr   Frederick Douglass   Rosa Parks
Langston Hughes   Walt Whitman   Sojourner Truth
Maya Angelou   Alice Walker
Thomas Merton   Jack Kerouac   David Amram   Harriet Tubman
Johnny & June Carter Cash   Tom House   Jimmie Rodgers
Bill Monroe   Woody Guthrie   Bob Dylan   Amiri Baraka
Gregory Corso   Lawrence Ferlinghetti   William Blake
Allen Ginsberg   Homer   Hunter S. Thompson   Dick Gregory
William Butler Yeats   James Joyce   William S. Burroughs
Joe Strummer   Pablo Neruda   Charlie Parker   Jackie Robinson
Vaclav Havel   Billie Holladay   Thelonius Monk   Christopher Felver
Zora Neale Hurston   Dizzy Gillespie   Lenny Bruce   Neal Cassady
Annie Wedekind   James Baldwin   Douglas Brinkley   John Beecher
William Carlos Williams   Toni Morrison   Diane di Prima
Anne Waldman   Miles Davis   Zoroaster   Ra
Buddha   Jesus   The Dalai Lama
Chogyem Trungpa Rinpoche   Pema Chodron   Edvard Munch
David Minton   Mother Teresa   Muhammad Ali and
The Holy Virgin Mary
surrounded by a host
of spirits we soared all the way
"all the way till the wheels
fell off and burned"
all the way to Louisville, Kentucky
to The Rudyard Kipling
at 422 West Oak Street where just
one hour ago we arrived we arrived to say welcome
welcome to this historic event
we are Keeping The Flame Alive
The Global Literary Renaissance
presents
this 31-hour non-stop music & poetry
10th Anniversary INSOMNIACATHON 2003
featuring
over 50 poets & writers

and over 40 bands & musicians
welcome   welcome   welcome
and here to officially kickoff INSOMNIACATHON 2003
Louisville's very own master of the
Montgomery, Alabama soul cryin
wounded heart blues
please welcome
the one and only Mr. Tyrone Cotton

Ron Whitehead
october 31, 2003
opening remarks
INSOMNIACATHON 2003
at The Rudyard Kipling

Searching For David Amram

    visited Putnam Valley
    flew to New York City   LaGuardia
    drove Bear Mountain   West Point   Peekskill
    then on to The David Amram Farm

welcome to Peekskill Hollow Road   Putnam Valley   New York

    wandered   side roads   main roads
        lost   for hours   dodging deer
        small suticase weighed down with
heavy words
    VIBRATIONS: A Memoir
    OFFBEAT: Collaborating With Kerouac
    David Amram's words his works his life
        autobiography
    he is spiritual intuitive psychic

"As I continued reading, I began to think that perhaps someday I would be able to write music that might have some of the quality that I felt in some of these writers I was beginning to admire more and more. I also thought from what I kept hearing in my head that my music could never take the route that composers were supposed to follow in 1955...I loved their music, but I was from Pennsylvania, not Vienna. I felt that if I was going to accomplish my dream, I would somehow have to write down what I felt and what I heard and hope that it would have enough impact to mean something to musicians who played it and eventually to people who would hear it."

    and I'm searching for David Amram
in Manitou   Highland Falls   Garrison Lake   Monegan
    New York City

"When Jack and I used to talk about his desire to find his lost Canadian-Indian heritage, I reminded him of the Navajo Prayer of the Twelfth Night. How the men and women prayed as they walked

on the trail of beauty. I sang him some of the old songs I had learned from Native American musicians. Jack and I both prayed in different languages, but the trail of beauty remained the same."

      welcome to New York   David Amram country
      I walked New York   into the wind
          rivers   mountains   sacred
       smokestacks   power plants   profane

and I'm searching for David Amram
    the greatest composer of them all
      he saves us from ourselves

and here I am in New York City
at the Casey Cyr Mike McHugh C Note Kerouac Amram Tribute
      who will save us now

and I'm searching for David Amram
    maybe Jack Kerouac can help
modern day prophet   from Lowell Massachusetts
    one of the great writers of all time

"Suddenly Dean stared into the darkness of a corner beyond the bandstand and said, "Sal, God has arrived."
I looked. George Shearing. And as always he leaned his blind head
    on his pale hand, all ears opened like the ears of an elephant, listening to the American sounds and mastering them for his own English summer's-night use. Then they urged him to get up and play. He did. He played innumerable choruses with amazing chords that mounted higher and higher
      till the sweat splashed all over the piano and everybody listened in awe

and fright. They led him off the stand after an hour. He went back to his dark corner, old God Shearing, and the boys said, "There ain't nothing left after that."

       maybe Allen Ginsberg   from Paterson New Jersey
       maybe Ginsberg can point the way
       with his "Howl" with his generous spirit

"I'm with you in Rockland
where we hug and kiss the United States under our bedsheets
the United States that coughs all night and won't let us sleep"

       maybe Gregory Corso   street poet from every street
       everywhere maybe Gregory Corso can help
       with his brutal honesty

"O Bomb I love you
  I want to kiss your clank eat your boom"

       I'm searching for David Amram   David Amram
       and the rivers of America
Merrimack, Hudson, Delaware, Susquehanna, Ohio, Kentucky,
Mississippi, Missouri, Colorado

       spray us with tears
       of immigrants
       who for forty days and forty nights have stood
       in the fields waited on the waters outside America's door
       knocking denied entry
       knocking on our doors pleading "let us come in"
       "let us live in your beautiful America"

       and I'm searching for David Amram

walking up hills   mountains   The Alleghenies   The Appalachians
The Rockies
                    bowing to gravity
     leaning backward with my long hair sweeping the path
        as I descend the wind and the descent flatten me
     and now my muscles are green and yellow and red pain
                sustaining my search
            drink red wine and strong coffee
                  at The C Note

          and I'm searching for David Amram

              I want love to have its way
         I want us to stand united   not divided
  One world One people   together   in peace and harmony

       and as I search for David Amram
       I sit in the C Note in New York City
       on a hot Saturday August 21st 2004
          drinking wine

            why do men still drink wine
            and women still water

beautiful people everywhere
and yes when I give readings round the world

I hear 3rd world voices monks and nuns

        Ernesto Cardenal   Nicanor Parra
        Daniel Berrigan   Thomas Merton
          Mother Teresa
             The Dalai Lama
pierce the world's terrors chanting singing praying
                          for love
                          for peace

        and I'm searching for David Amram
        "the one who'll shake the ones unshaken
        the fearless one"

      and searching for David Amram
      in the New York Public Library
   I looked in Lawrence Ferlinghetti's   yes San Francisco
Ferlinghetti who stood at Thomas Merton's grave with me
      Kentucky's Abbey of Gethsemani
   I look in Ferlinghetti's A CONEY ISLAND OF THE MIND and
                    PICTURES OF THE GONE WORLD
     and I read

  "Christ climbed down
    from His bare tree
    this year
    and softly stole away into
    some anonymous Mary's womb again
 where in the darkest night
    of everybody's anonymous soul
    He awaits again
    an unimaginable
    and impossibly
    Immaculate Reconception
    the very craziest
    of Second Comings."

       and I'm standing at the bar at the C Note
        lower east side New York City
         heart of New York
        on this beautiful Saturday August 21st 2004 night
        and the wind whispers
      welcome   welcome   welcome to New York to the C Note

  and I'm searching searching searching for Dave for David Amram
      searching for David Amram   in New York New York USA

closing time

from thingvellir Iceland we came, vikings,
crossed the atlantic in open vessel, wooden ship,

past a statue shouting empty words, liberty,
crossed the appalachian mountains to kentucky, hillbillies,

the viking hillbilly apocalypse revue, not knowing tour,
headed west into the canyoned night, west kansas in an old ford,

sarah sees people, spirits,
knocking pulling on our doors at 3am, rest stop,

depart further into deep night, shooting stars,
colorado sunrise boulder buddhist naropa, university,

did buddha suggest a university where was jesus' church,
wherever he was,
to woody creek hunter s thompson home, gonzo,

highway 133 backroads valleys mountain passes, telluride,
rosemerry and art goodtimes had by all, heart and lungs collapse,

climb mountains every one the last, america is an illusion,
america doesn't never did never will exist this poem is for nobody,
closing time,

tear down the fences that bound the prairies, the mountains,
saw down the parking meters the beaches long, everglades big sur,

take back the plundered earth hold it, heal it,
your bosom your womb embrace, take it back,

there are no boundaries no fences no owners, never were,
never will be only beauty this world is full, brimming,

pregnant with beauty los alamos, evil,
take it back the deserts, mojave,

the mountains the prairies the plains, take kansas please,
take it all back it is yours, we have tortured it long enough,

let us all go to spirit school until we are, healed,
ready to return to the vast purple green blue beauty, earth,

no name can describe the majestic beauty, of this place,
mother where is this we are here now but only, a little longer,

till closing time which is two or eight years, or days,
away places we traversed called, colorado new mexico arizona
california,

andy michael david james dean sarah, the heart of las vegas darkness,
mountain desert ocean deciduous evergreen, cactus,

a 2,700 sequoia years old largest living being, in the world,
where what place is this, why are we here,

except to live in peace harmony, not harm,
love embrace accept forgive grow our souls, be patient,

closing time has arrived, we had our chance,
and blew it, but thread of hope remains,

desert winds howling screaming, tumbleweed,
this poem is hope full, written by who,

this poem is for no borders, no boundaries,
this poem is for nobody, it is for,

this poem is for the deserts the mountains the oceans the forests,
majestic, this poem this closing time poem is for   nobody

From Jack Kerouac's Grave
to Forecastle 2006

Sarah and I were On The Road to
New York City to The Bowery Poetry Club

where we hooked up with David Amram and Casey Cyr
picked up Allen Ginsberg's and Gregory Corso's spirits and headed

on to Lowell Massachusetts
where we read and sang.

At sunset of the third day
we meditated on Jack Kerouac's grave.

I left a gift
a free Forecastle ticket on his tombstone.

I chanted an invitation to
the lonesome homesick traveler Jack Kerouac

Time was   Time is   Time will be no more
please come to

Forecastle 2006 please come
to the ending of time

and as I chanted   the wind moved the trees
they began to dance to sway

to the rhythmic sound of   chanting of
Time was   Time is   Time will be no more

please come to Forecastle 2006
and suddenly I felt a presence presences

as I chanted thanks to
all the bands to all the artists to all the environmental activists

to JK McKnight and everyone on the Forecastle Festival deck crew
to a global environmental renaissance

and as I chanted thanks
as kundalini energy moved through my body

I was lifted up up above
Jack Kerouac's grave up above the jade the emerald

blowing high summer leaves
up above the city of Lowell Massachusetts
and surrounded by presences

I recognize now as Jack Kerouac
James Joyce   Diane di Prima   William Carlos Williams

Rachel Carson   William Butler Yeats   Frederick Douglass
Chief Joseph   Walt Whitman   Thomas Merton   Robert Lax
Brother Patrick Hart   Velvet Underground

Henry David Thoreau   Ansel Adams   Maya Angelou
William Blake   Allen Ginsberg   Mother Jones
Derrick Jensen

William S. Burroughs   Herbert Huncke   Gregory Corso
Neal Cassady   Lawrence Ferlinghetti   David Amram
Hunter S. Thompson

Keep Louisville Gonzo   The Shinerunners   Anne Waldman
Ed Sanders   Amiri Baraka
Paul K & The Weathermen   Elizabeth Cady Stanton   Bjork
Randy Wayne White   Dylan Thomas
Toni Morrison   Will Oldham   Seamus Heaney   Jim James

Sylvia Plath Ken Kesey Kurt Vonnegut Casey Cyr
My Morning Jacket Megas Utangardsmenn

Jeffrey Scott Holland Scott Scarboro Andy Cook
Mark Reese Barbara Kingsolver Ed McClanahan
Bobbie Ann Mason Thomas Wolfe

James Still Jean Ritchie William Shakespeare John Prine
Robert Hunter Grandaddy
Hermann Hesse Jim Carroll Muddy Waters Knut Hamsun
Christopher Felver Nathanial

Townes Van Zandt Howlin Wolf Johnny Cash Billie Holiday
Ken Pyle Hank Williams Hound Dog Taylor Patsy Cline
Bill Monroe Richard Hell Sonic Youth

The Carter Family Billy Hardison Loretta Lynn
St. Francis John Cage Daddy

Woody Guthrie Lee Ranaldo Emmy Lou Harris Charles Bukowski
Gui Stuart Kurt Cobain Frank Messina

John Gage The Everly Brothers Raymond Render
Mose Rager Merle Travis Cameron Crowe Heart

Sigur Ros Sid Vicious Zoroaster Patti Smith Ra Jesus The Clash

Ramblin Jack Elliott Buddha Gandhi
Mother Teresa Edvard Munch Dylan Max

Milarepa Bob Dylan His Holiness The Dalai Lama Rumi
Rani Roz Mama Sarah and The Holy Virgin Mary

surrounded by a host
of spirits we soared all the way

"all the way till the wheels fell off and burned"
all the way to The Mellwood Arts & Entertainment Center

at 1860 Mellwood Avenue where just
minutes ago we arrived we arrived to say welcome

welcome to this historic event
Captain JK McKnight and his deck crew

present the 5th yes this is the 5th and the largest
largest Music Art and Activism Festival in the Midwest

Forecastle 2006   July 28th & 29th   11am to 11pm
featuring

25 bands, 59 artists and 30 environmental groups
welcome welcome welcome

and here to officially kickoff Forecastle 2006
well Stephen George of LEO said

"...her voice is deep and seductive...stunning and gorgeous...
majestic, elusive power...literary sensibilities...

a true Kentucky original."
she grew up in a cypress swamp

one mile from a nuclear plant
please welcome the beautiful glow in the dark mutant
Sarah Elizabeth

71

4
from Italy & Alabama to Kentucky & Beyond

Ron, North Sea, The Netherlands 1997, photo by Christopher Felver

Rant for international literary renaissance
Interview by Jordan Green

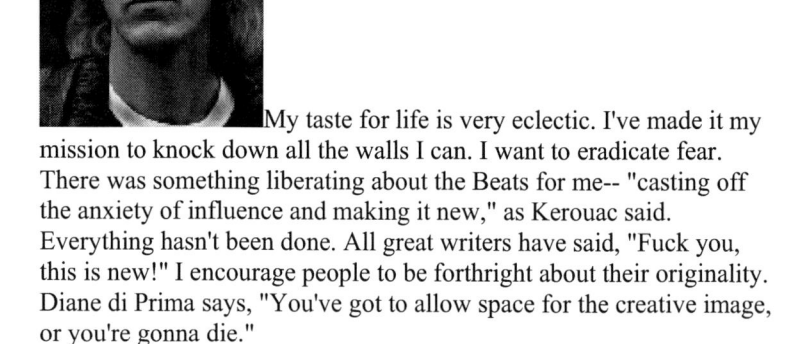

My taste for life is very eclectic. I've made it my mission to knock down all the walls I can. I want to eradicate fear. There was something liberating about the Beats for me-- "casting off the anxiety of influence and making it new," as Kerouac said. Everything hasn't been done. All great writers have said, "Fuck you, this is new!" I encourage people to be forthright about their originality. Diane di Prima says, "You've got to allow space for the creative image, or you're gonna die."

I grew up on a farm in Ohio County. My family is coal miners and farmers. My grandfather was a holy roller preacher. I worked for Kentucky Land Reclamation for awhile.

I ate a lot of speed in my youth. When I was in my teen years, I sat in a rocking chair-- rocking-- for four days. This will be written about in The Beaver Dam Rocking Chair Marathon. Another time I walked four days to raise money to take my family to the United Kingdom.

I talked everyone into putting money into an organization to promote poetry. This started as Thinker Review, a University of Louisville publication. Kent Fielding and I were hired by the board of directors to create a journal for U of L. The first thing I asked them was, "Can we turn this into the best in the world?" They thought we were too arrogant. We produced the first volume in six weeks. It was 465 pages. We wanted to create a literary renaissance from the start. We got our divorce from U o f L in May 1993 right after the Lawrence Ferlinghetti reading because U of L didn't like what we were doing. We did a hundred events a year. We'd get bands and poets to perform for free so that we could keep our costs down. We worked for free.

In March of '93 we had Eithne Strong and E. Ethelbert Miller scheduled for the same day. Our approach is to find performers and figure out how to pay for them later. We couldn't pay them so there was a mad scramble for money. Michael Crain and I came up with the idea of having an Insomniacathon. We booked Twice-Told Coffeehouse and put out the word for anybody who played an instrument or read poetry to come down and perform. Within hours it happened. Word just spread like wildfire. We raised money. We had to turn people away. That was the first night that Rodan played together. I think they played an acoustic set.

Your grandfather was a fundamentalist Baptist preacher or Pentecostal?

Holy roller. "Pentecostal" is kind of a formal way of stating it. Holy roller. "Holy" and "roller"-- both important words. They like to be called "holy roller" because that's what they did. They entered into this holy state of being, this communion with the holy spirit. They rolled on the floor. They spoke in tongues, some of them had seizures. They had visions. They had ecstatic experiences. Altered states of consciousness.

"Give me that church of the holy spook"
--Shane McGowan

Do you relate that to rock and roll?

Oh, I think so. People would dance on chairs with music playing loud: guitars, banjos, tambourines, pianos, people singing at the top of their voices. It's a way to vent all that sublimated energy-- sexual, spiritual, whatever-- to hopefully-- if you believe it-- to communicate it with, unite it with, consummate a relationship with your god. My God! That's like having some kind of sacred pleasure with God.

Did you get swept up in it when you were younger?

I got swept up in it from the point-of-view of the observer. I wasn't able to release that kind of energy until much later. The first inkling of that energy was when I saw Elvis Presley on the Ed Sullivan Show and my parents said, "Turn it off." That energy scared middle class America. But when I saw and heard the Beatles is when that electric energy-- just like a cattle prod-- you turn that thing on and stick a cow in the ass, they don't stand there, they jump. By God, that's what I did. I got up. I wanted to move. I had goose bumps all over me. The hairs stood up on the back of my neck. I was able to experience then, as a teenager, what the holy rollers experienced--what I witnessed as a child. We'd play ball at night down at the baseball park at Centertown (population 323) and they'd start singing up on the hill at the Holy Roller Church. Some of us boys would slip off and we'd walk up there and peek in the windows. Within an hour they'd be in their fits. I'll never forget the night my dad pulled up and told my brother and me, "Don't say anything." And we watched.

Was there some kind of break in your family when your dad rejected the Holy Rollers?

I don't know. Maybe my parents felt like the Holy Rollers were just too radical. They went to the other extreme in our community which was-- and most people'd laugh at this-- the Baptist Church. Some people think automatically-- Baptists, Holy Rollers, Pentecostal-- they're pretty similar, right? Well no, they're not. Baptists are kind of liberal compared to the Holy Rollers. And the other thing was, they went to the other extreme with their energy level. If anyone let out so much as a peep during the church service, fifty people turned around and stared you down. So I was shocked as a boy when finally-- this was when I was nine or ten-- I hadn't heard anything like this before- Matthew Tichenor brought his gospel quartet to our church. And Mrs. Duncan played on the piano like I'd never heard her before. She banged the hell out of that piano! I thought she was gonna tear it up. She was my third grade teacher and I'd never seen her behave like this in the classroom.

She was raising her arms up and slamming down on that piano. These guys sang their hearts out and I was excited about that gospel music.

My grand-dad on my mother's side was jack of all trades. He was a traveling musician as a young man, performed on radio stations across the country, played the banjo and the guitar. My mom and her sister, who were the two oldest of thirteen kids, sang with him on the radio many times. He had a couple restaurants he would set up in old buses he would fix up. He had a barber shop. He cut hair. He was a construction worker. His name was Raymond "Dick" Render. Some people called him the "Dixie Yodeler". He was a hell of a yodeler. He played kind of a combination of Woody Guthrie and Jimmie Rodgers- a real mixture of country and blues.

"What was all that noise about?"

He bought some ground down in western Kentucky and would go down there on weekends and clear the ground and try to fix it up. Also, the South End of Louisville was just growing at that time-- Valley Station, that area. This was in the '50's. He worked construction: he drove a grader and a bulldozer. He was the kind of person who just decided he could do whatever he set his mind to. So he worked a barbershop up here and did construction. He'd get off his construction job and go cut hair for two or three hours. Then he'd go down to western Kentucky on the weekends to work on the farm a couple of hours, then go into Centertown and cut hair. Then he'd get out and play basketball. He was kind of a wild man. He had Gypsy blood in him. He was going all the time.

We'd come up and visit Dick Render and his wife, Mamaw Lou Render. There were thirteen kids. Two had died when they were little, so there were eleven still living. The house was always packed. We'd sleep five or six in a bed. We'd get in a car-- there would sometimes be fifteen in a car. I'll never forget, at least twice, going around a curve and somebody would fall out. The door would pop open cause it was so packed. We were going probably 30 around a curve and my uncle,

Stevie, who was a year older than me, rolled out in a ditch. Luckily, there were leaves in the ditch. He rolled over in the ditch and jumped up. I looked back and we were yelling, "Stevie fell out! Stevie fell out!" We looked back, and he was up, jumping, yelling, "Hey, wait for me! wait for me!"-- running back to get in the car. And my grand-dad said, "Somebody hold on to that boy." And we took off again. There was always something like that happening. It was a lot of fun.

Then, when I was nine years old, my grand-dad was working on the first Watterson Expressway in 1959. And being the dare-devil that he was- he always thought he could do anything-- he had his grader on a slope that was too steep and he thought he could make it just fine, but it flipped over and landed on him. He lasted a week, but then he died. I've never seen, other than some celebrity on TV, a funeral where more people came. There were way over a thousand in the church and lined up both sides of the road outside the church.

That energy and excitement was part of what brought me to Louisville. I remember lying awake at night upstairs in their house and hearing the traffic on Dixie Highway-- the big trucks rumbling down the road all night long. On the road we lived on, at home in the country, there might be five or six cars come by all day. It was the kind of place where you could hear birds singing, a hawk high up the sky. The sounds of the city kind of drew me in. I knew that the city was the place for me. It was the sound of movement all night long. I mean, what was going on out there? What was all that noise about? Who would be up at that hour? I would wake up constantly in the night just imagining what might be happening. What are all those people doing out there still up?

Western Kentucky: late 1960's
What was your experience organizing coal miners in western Kentucky?

Well, my life was threatened. I worked for Peabody a couple times and then I worked for Kentucky Reclamation. I worked with a group of friends-- hard workers, hard-ass workers. This company had been formed to go in a reclaim-- (according to) the new laws that had been passed, the land had to reclaimed after it had been stripped. We had bulldozer operators go in and make hills-- you didn't have to flatten it out. Some of the steep cliffs we had to terrace. And on the terrace there would be enough width that you could back one of these huge trucks like a dump truck-- and I drove them-- you'd back it all the way down this long wall, some twice as long as a football field. You didn't have an inch to spare on the side and it was a straight drop down. Then you'd turn on your fertilizer. Then you'd fill up with seed and spread seed-- to grow grass, this real thick kind of fescue grass which was real strong and wouldn't rinse away and kept the ground from eroding. I'd do this all day-- just back up and down this damn cliff.

"If you're thinking about bringing in the union, you best be getting on out of here right now."

This company was not unionized, absolutely no benefits. It reminded me of chain gang labor. The foremen were complete jerks. They'd talk to their employees like they were worse than animals. I'm sure they treated their dogs much better. I'd never really seen anything like this before. I'd heard about it, I'd seen it in the movies. I was infuriated by it and I wanted to do something about it before I left. I did various jobs, drove these huge tractors that looked like monsters, that pulled ploughs and disks behind them. I did that, sowed seed, drove the big trucks, and did numerous other things. They also had tree planting crews. I finally decided that I had to begin a process towards unionization by getting all of the workers to agree to sign a petition asking for benefits like, for instance, over-time pay which they hadn't received up until then.

We'd go in sometimes at 4:30 in the morning and work until you couldn't see. The next day you'd go in, it'd rain and they'd send everybody home. No over-time, so you didn't have anything to depend on. I found out through one of the bosses how any changes might possibly be made. They said there was an annual meeting of the board of directors in St. Louis and any changes would have to be taken by the head of this local reclamation group. They had been doing this several years, no changes had been made, they weren't gonna make any changes. Everybody made minimum wage or a little bit more.

They weren't paid much of anything cause the company didn't have to. I typed up a letter, made it as formal as I possibly could, listed the benefits I wanted the employees to get. I started talking this up for a few days and one morning I went in earl y and convinced all 70 some of these men that this was the right thing to do and they all signed. I got them all in the warehouse before we went out on our day's work. I went into the boss' office, asked for all the bosses, the foremen, the supervisor to come in, said, "I have something to read." I climbed up onto a chair and read my petition. All the men applauded. Then everybody headed out to the trucks.

I was called into the office before I was allowed to leave. The supervisors were in there and they wanted to know what attorney had drawn this up because it sounded so professional. I told them I did it myself. Well, they didn't believe me. They wanted to know what group, what union was behind this. I said, "Absolutely none. I did all this myself." They let me go on to work. After lunch, my foreman come up to me and my cousin, he said, "I need to take y'all for a ride." He took us out away from everybody.

He said, "Look, I'm gonna tell you this. If anybody asks, I'm gonna say I never said anything or heard anything, but I want you to know that you better watch behind you all the time. People have been killed for doing less than what you done this morning." He said, "If you're thinking about bringing the union in here, you best be getting on out of here right now, and that's all I'm gonna say." Within a week the truck I was driving caught fire and blew up. Luckily I was able to jump out and roll away from the truck. But I was demoted from truck driver to pulling baby trees. I went out on that job one morning and-- driving the truck wasn't that bad, even on the bar pit wall-- but pulling those trees down on your knees all day-- I just knew already that I wasn't gonna do that. A truck was going in for supplies that morning and I hopped in the back of it. The foreman yelled at me, said, "Where the hell you think you're going?" I said, "I'm going to jack off. What's it to you?" I went on in and hitched a ride home. That was it for me.

I did hear from my cousin and my friends at work that a few months later after the next annual meeting-- since I was gone apparently they didn't feel threatened-- so a supervisor took my proposal to the annual meeting and had gotten those workers the benefits I'd asked for, so it made me feel really good. If I'd stayed there I don't think they would have even taken them cause they were suspicious that I was gonna bring the union in. But these guys did get some health benefits and over-time.

Originally published in *Blue Collar Boom: Honest Work*, Tilt-A-Whirl Press, August 1996.

From Italy to Kentucky & Beyond
Italy's Annalisa Papaleo interviews Ron Whitehead

December 2003

Annalisa: what do you think about American Literature today?

Ron: the best literature in Amerika today is coming from the Spoken Word scene. The Academic scene is boring, suburban, castrated, lifeless, cerebral, little Life Force.

Annalisa: which is your way to conceive literature in general?

Ron: the poet prophet (i.e. literature) deconstructs realism. she employs the innovative technique of intercalation: the juxtaposition of scenes in time. she is elus cohen, elect priest of expressionism, cubism, modernism, dadaism, surrealism, postmodernism but she is more. she is master alchemist, master magician. her long slender hand reaches towards me, grabs my throat, and pulls me into the book. manger du livre! I not only consume the book: the book consumes me.

Annalisa: do you think young generations are sensible to literature today?

Ron: yes. the most exciting global literary renaissance is occurring today with Spoken Word Poetry. my friend Lawrence Ferlinghetti told me City Lights Books, San Francisco, is selling more volumes of poetry than ever.

Annalisa: which are your favorite writers and why?

Ron: my favorite poet is Rumi then William Butler Yeats, followed by William Blake. there are many others whose work I drink daily. my favorite novelist is Knut Hamsun. there are many others whose work I drink daily. my favorite painters are Edvard Munch and David Minton. there are many others whose work I drink daily. "The Lake Isle of

Innisfree" is my favorite poem. HUNGER is my favorite novel. THE SCREAM is my favorite painting. THE SCREAM is the painting that best represents the human condition since Munch painted it in 1893. In the past 100 years we have murdered over 160 million people in one war after another. T. S. Eliot's "The Wasteland," 1922, is the poem that best represents the human condition in the first half of the 20th Century. Allen Ginsberg's "Howl," 1956, holds that position for the second half of the 20th Century. Jack Kerouac's ON THE ROAD, 1957, opened a door of consciousness. Hunter S. Thompson's FEAR AND LOATHING IN LAS VEGAS, 1971, closed that door. both are two of the most important novels of Amerikan Literature.

Annalisa: do you think to belong to any literary movement? which one? why?

Ron: I founded the Global Literary Renaissance with the goal of breaking down walls, of bringing people from round the world together. the pie, apple, is not limited, it is limitless. I want to work with everyone, even academics, suburbanites, ugh.

Annalisa: can you define which kind of poetry is yours?

Ron: I follow the muse. I have had several thousand pieces published in a diverse range of publications round the world. I write formal informal serious humorous political, love, zen, meditation, sex, Kentucky poems. whatever I am inspired to write. one of my goals in life is to break down as many walls and doors as possible. climb every mountain. forge every stream. trite and true.

Annalisa: which are the main themes of your poems?

Ron: the themes are as diverse as the poems. fearless compassionate honesty, non-violent fighting against injustice, life as it is, no disneyfication, no fundamentalist puritan whitewashing, terrible beauty.

Annalisa: what does it mean for you to be a writer?

Ron: everything! being a poet is an innate drive that seizes a human being and makes her or him its instrument. the poet is not simply a person acting freely, in pursuit of a merely private end, but one who allows poetry/art to realize its purposes through her or his person. poets/artists/writers/filmmakers have moods, free will, personal aims, but as poets they are bearers of a collective humanity, carrying and shaping the common unconscious life of the species. if history is the embodiment of "fear, reason, social convention, and tradition" then it becomes the duty, the responsibility, the compelling creative urge of the nabi, the prophet, the poet to crack history's encrusted, iconostasic, shell releasing the dying and dead by invocation of The Word, inspired thought energy into meaning full sound. the prophet becomes poet, which in greek means creator, and as poet, whose home is in shadow in the holy unholy realms of The Creative Imagination, as the synaptic link between spirit and matter, creates a new world.

Annalisa: we are talking about literature but how important is music for you in a literary work and why?

Ron: Vico suggests that "the human mind does not understand anything of which it has had no previous impression from the senses." sensory meditations experiences move the poet prophet to another level of translation. movement through space creates time, a stride at a time, now. awareness of being in space involves the sensory act of seeing, the "ineluctable modality of the visible" (Joyce). movement creates time and initiates hearing. i am space, moving, step by step, creating time. i am. i create myself and all that i experience, every moment as i move through my self-created space creating time. space and time. static and kinetic. movement through space creates time. magic and instinct shape movement into rhythm. rhythm measures time. movement/rhythm is active, action, kinetic, causality.
movement may be monotonous buy rhythmic movement is creative. rhythm breathes energy into form. a perpetual poetic world is in the making. the marriage of the creative polarities of form and energy, space and time, is consummated by movement, rhythmic movement. music is central to all my writing, to my poetry, to life.

Annalisa: which is your bigger ambition as a writer?

Ron: to help make the world a better, friendlier, safer, more honest, open, accepting world in which to live.

Annalisa: any dreams?

Ron: i have been living my dream for thirteen years. everything now is icing on the cake. life is an exciting adventure. i hope to spend the rest of my life traveling the world sharing poems music with everyone i meet.

Annalisa: what have you got in common with The Beat Generation?

Ron: much. it has been my honor to be friend, editor, publisher, organizer, and to read with many members of the so-called Beat Generation. today specialization is sold on every corner, fed in every home, brainwashed into every student, every young person. we are told that the only way to succeed, here at the beginning of the 21st Century is to put all our time, energy, learning, and focus into one are, one field, one specialty (math, science, computer technology, business). If we don't we will fail. We are subtly and forcefully, implicitly and explicitly, encouraged to deny the rest of who we are, our total self, selves, our holistic being. The postmodern brave new world seems to reside inside the computer via The Web with only faint peripheral recognition to the person, the individual (and by extension the real global community), the real human being operating the machine. The idea of and belief in specialization as the only path, only possibility, has sped up the fragmentation, the alienation which began to grow rapidly within the individual, radically reshaping culture, a century ago with the birth of those Machiavellian revolutions in technology, industry, and war. And with the growing fracturing fragmentation and alienation comes the path - anger, fear, anxiety, angst, ennui, nihilism, depression, despair - that, for the person of action, leads to suicide. Unless, through our paradoxical leap of creative faith, we engage ourselves in the belief, which can become a life mission, that, regardless of the consequences, we can, through our engagement, our actions, our loving life work, make the world a better, safer, friendlier place in which to live. Sound naive? What does this have to do with The Beat Generation? with the youth of today? what place does the antinomian voice, the voice of The Beat Generation, the voice that, though trembling, speaks out against the powers that be, what place does this outsider voice have in the real violent world in which we are immersed? are we too desensitized to the violence to even think it worthwhile to consider the possibility of a less violent world? are we too small, too insignificant to make any kind of difference? the power-mongers have control. what difference can one little individual life possibly make possibly matter? today the X and microserf generations are swollen with young people yearning to express the creative energies buried in their hearts, seeping from every pore of their beings. They ache to change to heal the world. is it still possible? is it too late? is there anyone (a group?) left to show the way to be an example? to be a guide? a mentor? James Joyce, King of Modernism, said the idea of the hero was nothing but a damn lie that the primary motivating forces are passion and compassion. as late as 1984 people were laughing at George Orwell. Today, as we finally move into an Orwellian culture of simulation life on the screen landscape, can we remember passion and compassion or has the postmodern ironic satyric deathinlifegame laugh killed both sperm and egg? is there anywhere worth going from here? is it any wonder that today's youth have adopted Jack Kerouac, Allen Ginsberg, William S. Burroughs, Herbert Huncke, Gregory Corso, Neal Cassady, Lawrence Ferlinghetti, Amiri Baraka, Robert Creeley, David Amram, Diane di Prima, Ed Sanders, Anne Waldman, Bob Dylan, and all the other Beat Generation and related poets, writers, artists, musicians as their inspirational, life-affirming antinomian ancestors? These are people who have stood and still stand up against unreasoning power/right/might, looked that power in the eyes and said NO i don't agree with you and this is why. and they have spoken these words not for money or for fame but out of life's deepest convictions, out of the belief that we, each one of us, no matter our skin color our economic status our political religious sexual preferences, all of us have the right to live to dream as we choose rather than as some supposed higher moral authority prescribes for us.

Annalisa: what do you like or dislike with Beats?

Ron: i like their life-affirming inclusiveness.

Annalisa: and what do you agree or not?

Ron: i disagree with their exclusivity.

Annalisa: who is your favourite Beat artist?

Ron: there is much i like, admire, respect about all of them. Kerouac is one of the great writers of all time. Ginsberg's "Howl" and "Kaddish" are as good as any poems written by any other American poets. Corso is one of Amerika's truly original poets. Burroughs, like Swift, is one of the most politically astute writers of all time. Ferlinghetti's poems get better and better. he is one of my favorite poets. Bob Dylan is the greatest songwriter of all time, and a great singer. David Amram, one of Amerika's alltime great composers, is my favorite.

Annalisa: what do you think about that Kerouac and others believe that literature has to be accompanied also to music?

Ron: the greatest literature is music.

Annalisa: do you feel a beat?

Ron: always.

Annalisa: what does the word Beat mean to you? do you agree with Kerouac's definition of it?

Ron: yes i agree with everything Kerouac said about the word Beat.

Annalisa: critics have always been very hard with the Beats considering them just a group of tossic or rebels. According to you, why in their times have they not been understood?

Ron: in the next decade The Beats will come to be recognized as the most important group of poets and writers in the history of Amerika. The Beats have given birth to new generations to new energies which are awakening to the realization that the creative imagination provides salvation from suicide, from death in life, by revealing that there are alternative paths to explore in this world alternative paths that lead away from the mundane, the superficial, away from submission to mediocrity alternative paths opening into the inspired fire called Life. the hallowed doors of academia, academia, the bastion of conservative thought, the doors of academia are finally creaking open (just as it took so long for them to open to James Joyce, Virginia Woolf, Samuel Beckett & all other original thinkers and expressionists) the doors are creaking open, and, finally, at least a discourse on The Beats has begun.

Annalisa: do you think The Beats still exist?

Ron: yes.

Annalisa: what can we find of Beats in America today?

Ron: Lawrence Ferlinghetti, David Amram, Diane di Prima, Amiri Baraka, Ed Sanders, Anne Waldman, Bob Dylan, Ron Whitehead, & others.

"An Interview with Ron Whitehead" by Foster Dickson
for the *Evergreen Review*

Seeing Ron Whitehead for the first time, he immediately gives the impression that he is either an old hippie or someone you really wouldn't want to mess with. Standing well over six feet tall, he wears his hair long, down his back, with its mix of blond and gray, and a beard that is wispy and gray that extends about a foot down his chest. He usually dulls his intense blue eyes behind rimless, round glasses, giving him the feel of someone who is older than his fifty-four years. Typically, Ron wears loose fitting pants and a long-sleeved button-down shirt, almost always with the sleeves rolled down and the top button done, which hides his numerous, colorful tattoos. Ron Whitehead looks like your wise old grandpa gone awry.

I rode up from Montgomery, Alabama to Louisville, Kentucky to see Ron and his wife Sarah in late March, the week after the vernal equinox, as the trees and fields of Tennessee and Kentucky were only beginning to peek through with green over the deadness of the winter. I knew Ron from working a few years earlier on a poetry book of another non-mainstream Nashville poet, Tom House, and then invited Ron down to Montgomery to read his poems at the New South bookstore I was also working in at the time. That was the first time I also met Sarah Elizabeth, then not yet his wife, a twenty-something Kentucky singer-songwriter with long brown hair reminiscent of a 1970s Emmylou Harris and with a vocal style to match. What began as Ron alone turned into Ron and Sarah, then quickly escalated into a performance by his on-again/off-again group, The Viking Hillbilly Apocalypse Revue, which added in an aging Icelandic guitarist, Michael Pollack, and a younger percussionist/didgeridoo player, Andy Cook. The group is a hodge-podge of personalities and styles that mixes and matches country and bluegrass music, Beat poetry, world rhythms, and a politically conscious sing-along. As I climbed the Cumberland plateau after passing through northern Alabama, I thought about that weekend that the crew had invaded my house. It had been more than a year, and Ron had immortalized those two days in his poem, "From Hank Williams' grave to Insomniacathon 2003: Keeping the Flame Alive".

Arriving in Louisville, a thriving city of about one million people, I headed for The Highlands, the colorful neighborhood where the Whitehead's live. The Highlands is an old neighborhood of tall, ancient trees and large, distinctive houses that has become an intermingling of bourgeois nostalgia for the past, wealthy families, and a neo-hippie bohemian element that congregates in a shopping, restaurant, and music district that is centered around Bardstown Road. Ron and Sarah fall into the latter of the three categories. Passing by a statue of Daniel Boone at the main entrance to Cherokee Park, Louisville's largest park, I found their small apartment building not far off the main drag. I walked through the bright red front door and through a series of landings and up to the stale heat of the third floor, apartment #10. Ron answered the door with my glass of red wine, already poured, in his hand.

After a catching up over those glasses of afternoon wine, we grabbed some dinner at a nearby restaurant. After we had eaten and Ron and I had a couple more glasses each, Sarah proclaimed that we seemed riled up enough to go home and get started.

FD: Since you don't really consider yourself a Southern writer, it seems to me that the Beats play a pretty big role for you. When did you discover the Beats, or if not that, what led you to them?

Ron: Well, you know, I've had many major influences in my life. I've had mentors. I've had a lot of good English teachers, the earliest being my preacher's wife who took me under her wing when I was a boy; she saw something in me. She turned me on to so many books I may not have ever read. But my grandfather Whitehead, the holy roller preacher, he inspired me. My granddad Render, the musician, inspired me. My parents, as I said, inspired me in their own ways. The first time I heard a gospel quartet in my church, man, I was lifted off the ground. I love that music. And when I heard Elvis Presley on the Ed Sullivan

Show, that lit a fire under my ass. I got goosebumps all over me. When I saw the Beatles on Ed Sullivan, then started listening to WLS radio, 890 AM, out of Chicago every night. . . . and WLS played all the latest cutting edge rock songs in the early sixties, so that inspired me and that was a big impact on me. Bob Dylan was, early Bob Dylan, was a major influence. And still is. And then I was turned on to poetry, to Rumi, the 12th century Sufi mystic poet, who I love to this day. He was a radical in every way. To Kahlil Gibran's The Prophet. When I was 16, a friend gave it to me, and said, you have got to read this. I had gone to her with several questions about the New Testament. What about this? Can you answer this? And she couldn't answer any of the questions. She just always said, "Now, Ronnie, there are some things we don't need to ask, we just need to accept 'em." When she gave me The Prophet by Gibran, she said, "this is dangerous." One thing led to another. And as a teenager I began to travel to Louisville by Greyhound Bus, and then by motorcycle, and then I bought a car for fifty dollars, spray painted it silver – bought twelve cans of spray paint to cover the rust. And then I drove to Louisville in it. Over 100 miles away from our farm. And there was a bookstore in downtown Louisville, W. K. Stuart's. I went there on my visits. I bought fifteen or twenty books, depending on how much money I had, all paperbacks of course. I just started reading— I joined book clubs when I was a little boy, because I realized that the mail came everyday, and the mail could bring stuff from anywhere in the world. My parents subscribed to a few magazines like Reader's Digest, and so I went through and looked at 'em, and I started seeing— and I started reading avidly, which I've done all my life. So somewhere in my teens I came across Jack Kerouac. And it was about that the time the whole hippie thing was going on, San Francisco was going on, the Vietnam War was going on. Lots of books and photos and literature was coming out about the Holocaust. I had already been going through, and in school they had been showing films of the atomic, and the nuclear thing that was going on. And so as a little boy I woke up with nightmares, just drenched with sweat, having a dream about the nuclear wind coming and blowing down our home and killing our entire family. We were all dying in that recurring dream. So then I started reading about the Nazi concentration camps, the Jewish Holocaust, and I remember lying on my bed, crying, crying, crying. I couldn't believe that it was possible for people to do this sort of thing to each other. And so from the age of thirteen – I think, all my life but thirteen is when I really started – diving into this other world that I dwelt in. I started reading other kinds of literature, and Kerouac touched a chord in me, as did J. D. Salinger, as did John Steinbeck. I read <u>Grapes of Wrath</u> when I was in high school. It tore me completely up. I cried like a baby when I read that book. And so Steinbeck is one of my favorite writers. <u>Grapes of Wrath</u> is one of my favorite books of all time. I consider Kerouac and Steinbeck to be two of the greatest— maybe the two greatest writers in America, both. They wrote about the downtrodden, the down-and-out, the people who struggled, who suffered, who put it all on the line and didn't always make it. And I love those writers. So you combine that with the kind of upbringing that I had, I mean, that was my experience. My dad was a union coal miner – and let me tell you something – if you don't know about John L. Lewis, I grew up learning about John L. Lewis, the formation of unions in America. The fights, the deaths in the working class, the ones who sacrificed their lives in order to get better working conditions for millions of people— I mean, the U.S. Army was called out to bomb work camps in eastern Kentucky during the formation of coal miners unions, so it was literally a war. It was a war. When I was growing up this was serious, serious shit. When the UMWA, United Mine Workers Association, went out on strike, people were shot and killed. Where I grew up people were shot and killed. So when I read these stories, about the people, about the Okies, because of the Dust Bowl, they had to leave their homes in Oklahoma and go to California, and pick fruit from trees and get brutally beaten by the owners of these big farms, you know man, I'm right there with 'em, because I saw it happening, in my own world. And with Kerouac, I read about the hoboes, the downtrodden, the down-and-out, I understood why people turned away from big government, big corporations, plantation owners. I understood <u>Huckleberry Finn</u> by Mark Twain, why people wanted to escape from all that and just float on down the river. Just get in a car and travel and leave it all behind. Yeah, I understood, and I understand it to this day. I can't stand injustice, people hurting other people. I understand people treating people fairly . . . That's what I understand. These writers – the Beats and others who are, I think, spiritually connected, who inspired the Beats – well, I'm on the same page with them. And I want to carry on that tradition of telling the stories, writing the poems, of the downtrodden, the down-and-out class. Those who are struggling . . . I'm for those people. But those who have need to share with those who have-not. So that's why I'm drawn to the Beats. The Beatitudes. Beat means not only downtrodden, beat down by the system and society, but as Kerouac pointed out— he said to be beat is to be spiritual, beatific, beatitude.

FD: In the poem, "Sex Education," the father refers to the speaker, who is presumably you, as "Bone". As well, this figure composed of a stacked circle, triangle and square. What do you mean when you talk about "Bone" or the "Bone Man"?

Ron: Okay, well, I happen to take after my granddad Render, my mom's dad, and he's built like me. Tall, thin, muscular. My dad and my brother are built more like Hercules. My dad is six foot and my brother five-ten. Both are muscular, about two hundred pounds. And I was always wanting to be the leader, never wanting to be told what to do, I had to compete and stay up with them. And with anybody else who was attempting to lead the way. So it was something that just came to me. I didn't really have the confidence to come out of the closet as a poet at seventeen, because I was already getting enough ass-beatings as it was. I chose not to say anything about it. So what happened was I chose to develop – I had to develop – a whole other world inside myself. So I created some characters and decided to call myself the "Bone Man." And my brother, the "Muscle Man". And my invisible older brother, the "Brain Man". . . and so in my studies, I've gone through periods in my life when I've read as many as three books a day, doing research, studying, digging deeper into the meaning of life, searching for answers. And I studied Zoroastrianism. I've studied all the world religions and all the different spiritualities, and Zoroastrianism for a while, and I came across this symbol. The circle under which is the square under which is the triangle, and I decided to start signing that figure after my name, and it is the ancient Zoroastrian symbol for a human being. The circle represents love, the square power, and the triangle wisdom. It's those three *in balance* that creates the ideal human. It's a state toward which we continually strive, hopefully, if we're awake enough, and want to fulfill our potential, then we're striving toward the balance of love, power and wisdom. If one overrides too much, you're out of balance. But that's what that symbol means to me. And I am the Bone Man. The Bone Man dances circles round the subterranean gloom, paints pink and blue and purple until he fills the room with the smell of roses, and a pandemonium moon. I want to create beauty. I want to find happiness, but this is a strange world we live in, and I like Jonathon Swift's saying, "Vex the world." I think it's good to constantly pull the rug out from under ourselves. Not just the world, but ourselves. One of my goals in life is to move beyond all fear. And part of that process is facing, embracing, and therefore being able to move beyond fear, is to be able to go where there is no ground. So I choose to walk on groundlessness, in openness.

FD: Okay, I want to talk a little more about your work now, about individual poems. Tell me about the poem "Tapping My Own Phone".

Ron: (*laughing*) Well, you're gonna get some insight. I don't know that I've given this information publicly. I only told a handful of people privately, but why not . . . well, in the mid-nineties – and it's a blur – the last fifteen years is a blur . . . I published 600 titles and I decided early on I wanted to call them "Published in Heaven", because in Allen Ginsberg's Howl— William Carlos Williams wrote the foreword or the introduction to "Howl". Ginsberg named a handful of books, written by his friends – Burroughs and Kerouac and Cassady – he said all these books are published in heaven. I loved that. I loved it. So I talked with him one time – I worked with Ginsberg the last five years of his life – and we had a real dynamic working relationship . . . but I published about 600 titles: books, posters, chapbooks, CDs. Two of the 200 posters I produced are posters of poems by and photos of President Jimmy Carter. After Lincoln, Carter is my next favorite president, and I feel like the reason Carter didn't achieve anymore than he did as

President was because he was so honest. He told it like it was. He didn't play the game. He was sabotaged every step of the way during his entire term as President. He left looking bad in the public eye. Not in my eyes. I knew he was a poet, and I wanted to publish him. I wanted to include him in the series. The only two people I haven't included that I want to include in the series are Bob Dylan and Muhammad Ali. But I got the Dalai Lama, and I thought, I want to include Jimmy Carter. So I met Doug Brinkley [skipping over] . . . and we produced the New Orleans Insomniacathon in 1996 [skipping over] . . . that was an amazing year . . . well, I told Doug— I produced a poster by Doug, "Dehydrated Dawns in the Cafe du Monde" [skipping over] . . . Doug knows everybody. So Doug got the assignment to write the new biography of President Jimmy Carter. Now, I'm getting to "Tapping My Own Phone". I had to tell you that about Doug, it's important. So Doug's writing the Carter biography. It's intense. He had to go through the highest levels of security clearance of the U.S. government to be allowed to go into the Presidential archives . . . so Doug liked my idea, and he had opened the doors for me to get these two poems and photos for two posters by President Jimmy Carter. So I produced them. When I move on something, I move! . . . Most of the people I publish I deal directly with the people, but not all of 'em. So I sometimes need an intermediary and in this case I have one. Now, I'm teaching at U[niversity] of L[ouisville] . . . in 1995. One more morning, I'm cleaning up getting ready to head out the door to go teach at the University of Louisville, and the phone rings. And it's Doug Brinkley. And he's in an undisclosed location— he says, I can't tell you . . . outside of Plains, Georgia. And I can tell by the tone in his voice that's he panicked. He says, Ron . . . you have got to call this number RIGHT NOW! There is going to be a Secret Service SWAT Team, there are going to be helicopters landing on your house in a matter of minutes if you don't get this cleared up RIGHT NOW! The posters have arrived at Carter's— Presidents have this public office and people working there, and they also have a private office and people working there— Doug had given me the address and the name of the private secretary and office, and that's where I shipped President Carter's posters to. The posters arrived . . . they didn't know me from anybody. They didn't know these packages were comin'. Ex-Presidents receive – I found out through this process – about five thousand pieces of mail everyday. And they have a whole army of people who screen that mail, because that mail includes a certain number of death threats. So it's high level stuff. But the box of posters I shipped arrived, they didn't go through any of that preliminary screening. They just went right to this secret, magical destination. Well, Secret Service agents are on the phone immediately. They got the bomb team out. They're circling, holding all the equipment over the boxes. They finally, with their gloves on and everything, open the boxes, slice the end open – everybody's got all the equipment on . . . and they slide out one of the posters, and thank God they see Doug's name on there with my name! They know Doug and they call him first. And Doug says, you wouldn't believe what I've had to go through, and he tells me the whole story FAST! . . . and you have got to tell them that you did all this on your own! And say whatever you need to say to get the heat off me, I've got to finish this book project, I'm nearly done, so you gotta help me out here. And I said okay, and while Doug's on the phone I hear helicopters. And not just one, there are four helicopters flying over my house! . . . And so I called this number, and I told them who I was, and I explained the situation, and I apologized. And Carter's secretary said, I don't have ANY record of this! Who gave you authorization to do this? the secretary told me, you're gonna go to court, and you're gonna have problems, and you got a lot of explaining to do! . . . the word that I finally got was that Carter absolutely loved the posters. So, out of that was born the poem, "Tapping My Own Phone". It was a horrifying experience. (*And with that, he begins to laugh, again.*) I thought it was all over . . .

FD: Alright, another of your signature works is "I will Not Bow Down". Tell me about that one.

Ron: Well, I consider myself to be on a spiritual journey. I'm here. I believe in reincarnation. I believe that I'm here to grow my soul. I have chosen the bodhisattva path. In other words, I've taken a vow to myself. I'm not a member of any religion. My only religion is love.

That's it. And I'm a spiritual person, not a religious person. The bodhisattva path is one that in which you make the choice to reincarnate until all beings have achieved enlightenment, are awake, are happy, and so that's the path I'm on. I'm attempting to wake up. I want to uplift and inspire through my life and my work, anybody and everybody I can. One thing my parents taught me was never to look up to or down at anybody. Look everybody eyeball to eyeball, shoulder to shoulder, we're all in this together. I've studied all the world religions, and I feel most drawn to Native American and Tibetan Buddhist spiritualities. In my studies of the Bible, I have been most deeply inspired in the Old Testament by the book of Daniel and in the New Testament by the book of John. I taught the book of Daniel and it was after many close readings of that book, and in my politics, that "I Will Not Bow Down" was born. It's one of those poems that was a long time comin'. I tend to write in my head, construct poems, stories, songs, books, whole books in my head, process 'em, and when I get to the point that I put pen and ink to paper, it tends to flow quickly. Then I tend to go back and revise and edit. But "I Will Not Bow Down" was inspired by the book of Daniel and my deep anti-authoritarian sentiments and my deep yearning to heal the Earth – and I consider that all of us are part of Mother Earth . . . I think, if you live that way, that's love, that's the path of love. honor all beings. That's what that poem's about. It's about resistance, dissent against injustice, it's about healing. The poem is all about America. America was born out of dissent. America is based on the principle that all beings have equal rights. That poem is about healing. That's it.

FD: Alright, then, what's your favorite poem that you've written?

Ron: I have— I can't name a favorite.

FD: A couple of favorites?

Ron: I have so many favorites, and, you know, the whole Zen prayer-meditation series of poems that I did, like "The Shape of Water" and "Listen" and "Plowed Earth", those are so meaningful to me. My poems— I believe in the power of going beyond, keep going beyond 'til you break through to the other side, and sometimes sensory deprivation helps in that process. In the Beaver Dam Rocking Chair Marathon where I stayed up and rocked in a rocking chair for eighty-nine hours and fifty-five minutes, Saturday morning to Wednesday morning was one of those breakthrough periods. I've discovered there are different times in my life when I have reached about when I'm near breakdown that the veil between worlds disappears. Things come to me. Like when I met the Dalai Lama, and I've met him several times, in both waking moments and in lucid waking dreams. When I received the poem, "Never Give Up," when the Dalai Lama was giving me the message . . . If I don't do anything but share that poem, "Never Give Up", with people the rest of my life it would have been worth it . . . But "I Will Not Bow Down", "Tapping My Own Phone", "Mama", "Sex Education", "Gimme Back My Wig: The Hound Dog Taylor Blues", those are important poems to me. Some of my most requested, and some of my most often published poems.

FD: You mentioned it, but that's my next one: "The Shape of Water".

Ron: "The Shape of Water". You know, I— Meditation has been such a blessing to me. Drugs. In my travels The Netherlands is the most civilized country I've been to. I think we could learn much by modeling our own country after the Netherlands. I think as adults we should have the right to choose how to live our lives, as long as we're not hurting other people. And I think that drugs, for some people, can be doorways to spiritual realms. They were for me. Many Native Americans took peyote or mescaline once a year as part of their religious ritual. The shaman will take those drugs as often as necessary to communicate with the other side, with the spiritual realms . . . but I started studying meditation many years ago. I've gone places. And the Zen prayer-meditation poems I mentioned earlier – "The Shape of Water" is one – I started contemplating and meditating on the vastness of the mind. How vast is the mind? We have no idea. And I believe in this theory, I came up with this theory, called the Ocean of Consciousness, which I wrote a book about. And I think that beyond Post-Modernism, beyond chaos theory, there is an ocean of consciousness. There is truth. There is form. Beyond chaos. You see, chaos is just another illusion. So I just started questioning the shape of mind. And then I thought about, well, in the same breath, what is the shape of water? How can we determine the shape of water? Because water manifests in so many different ways. Mind does too. So that poem is a contemplation of mystery, paradox and uncertainty.

FD: We've talked about religion a fair bit. We've talked about the path of the bodhisattva and that You don't subscribe to any particular religion. On your website, you have several pictures of yourself at Thomas Merton's grave, who is a particularly religious poet. Tell me about that.

Ron: Catholic . . . The spiritual path I have chosen, I'm more of a yogi, a wild man, and by choice. I can't comply with – I don't want to comply with – any system, any rigid system or practice. I take from many practices what works best for me in my own life and change it as I feel the need to change it . . . Thomas Merton, I came to Catholicism through Irish literature. Years ago, Gene Williams and I owned and operated an underground bookstore I named For Madmen Only, after a magic theater in Herman Hesse's <u>Steppenwolf</u>. and right next door we had The Store, which was a head shop. And we sold books by the Beat Generation, Dostoevsky, Thomas Merton, & others. I consider Thomas Mertion and Mother Teresa, within the Catholic Church, to best exemplify what it means to be a Christian. Because Merton, like Jesus, was a radical and he wanted change in the Church. All churches need change. I wouldn't bat an eye if all formal religions ended in this instant. There would be no tears shed here. Mother Teresa fed and clothed the poor. Thomas Merton questioned everything and in his three meetings with The Dalai Lama he inspired The Dalai Lama to become more ecumenical in his view, embracing and being more open to all the world religions. Merton was one of the most brilliant writers and thinkers in history. Seven or eight volumes of his journals were published in the last handful of years . . .he sat down at night and wrote. master writers work for years to write the way he wrote . . . Full of life.

He loved to drink. Loved jazz! I was fortunate enough to publish Merton, a poster and a chapbook. It was James Laughlin, founder of New Directions, who gave me the poem to publish, and it was Ron Seitz who wrote "Song for Nobody" about his friendship with Merton who gave me the photo. they had many stories about things they and Merton did.

FD: You've talked about Thomas Merton, an Irish Catholic, and The Dalai Lama, a Tibetan Buddhist, and that brings me to my next question. You have on your website the Global Literary Renaissance. What is that?

Ron: On February 4, 1992, with Kent Fielding, I started a literary renaissance in Louisville. Kent and I were hired to be editors of what had been the University of Louisville's student literary publication. I asked the board— they asked me if I was willing to be co-editor with Kent – I was finishing up graduate work, getting ready to start teaching – I started teaching in August 1992– I asked them if I had their permission to turn this into one of the best international arts publications. The entire board looked at me and laughed real loud, of course, but that's what I proceeded to do: to start a renaissance in Louisville. And I said, yeah I definitely want to do that, but my view is to start a global literary renaissance – and Kent thought that was real funny, too – but that's what I proceeded to do. So a year later I left, after much tension, after unbelievable tension, fights and battles, and I left the University of Louisville after I taught there for five years. At Lawrence Ferlinghetti's suggestion I created a new non-profit organization called The Literary Renaissance. I wanted to create a community of like-minded individuals, everybody doing their own unique work, to come together as a team, as friends, as a family, as a community, to build and maintain a network of creative musicians, poets, writers, artists and filmmakers all over the world. We would collide and come together whenever possible in these temporary autonomous zones called Insomniacathons, usually, but also in different manifestations. Like the Meer dan Woorden More Than Words Festival in the Netherlands, a ten-day international arts festival I produced with Jan Pankow and others in the Netherlands. The LIPS Festival – London International Poetry and Song Festival – I produced with Richard Deakin in London England. The others just on down the line. And to make it a real, living, breathing community that grows, and I've been doing that since February 4, 1992. But especially since April of 1993 when I separated myself— I gave a talk with Lawrence Ferlinghetti at the University of Louisville, and I separated myself from the University. I intentionally went global, but I had started at the University of Louisville. Diane Di Prima was the first one in . . . simultaneously within the same week I brought Lucien Stryk in . . . he was the second poet, and for three years – even when I separated myself from U of L – I went throughout Louisville and Kentucky to produce three, four, five events per week. Two, three, four new titles per month. And I led that attack. The streets were on fire in Louisville then. That's when the literary renaissance was born. Now people who were inspired by those days are starting to produce their own work, their own events, their own CDs. It's something that has grown all over the planet.

FD: As a poet you seem to fall into the Beat generation in terms of style but your age would put you into what most Americans would call the hippie generation. However, you seem to have accepted modern technology and its uses with a more youthful vigor than many older artists and writers. In terms of a generation, how do you see yourself?

Ron: You know, I've studied that, and I'm between generations. I've always accepted all generations because of the way I grew up in Kentucky. I grew up around an eccentric array of people all ages, all dynamic personalities. And so I've always felt ageless. I've always felt youthful and ancient at the same time. So I embrace the Beats, I embrace the hippies, I embrace the punks. I continue to feel the closest kinship with the hippies, because the hippies – I believe – are reincarnated Atlantians who are spiritual brothers to the Native Americans and the Buddhists. I've been attracted and drawn to those people all my life. If you look at the Tibetans and you look at the Native Americans they look alike, their skin colors are the same, their spiritualities are so similar. I've always felt at one with them. And as to the technology thing, I have believed all my life that we can have the best of both worlds, that we can use technology, that we don't have to live as primitives. We can live in harmony with nature, utilizing modern technology in a harmonious way. Sarah and I and the Viking Hillbilly Apocalypse Revue last year did this two-month U.S. Tour and we visited Dan Roberts in northern California. Dan lives in a self-sufficient, solar-powered home in a redwood forest. Man, I love that! That's the way we want to go! . . . I used to be one of those – I forget what they're called – anti-machine. I hated computers. Then in '94, NYU asked me to produced a 48-hour, non-stop music and poetry Insomniacathon to kick off NYU's 50-year celebration of The Beat Generation . . . it takes so much time and effort, months in advance, to produce an event like that, and so the phone bills were four thousand dollars a month! And Lee Ranaldo [of the band, Sonic Youth] said, Ron, you have got to use e-mail. And I said, aw I hate computers, and so I asked Ferlinghetti about it, and he said fuck computers, man. But after the NYU New York Insomniacathon, when my power was off for six months because I had such high phone bills I said I'm going to check out this email thing when I come out of all this, and it has saved me thousands of dollars a month!

NAKED INTERVIEW

CONVERSATIONS WITH WILLIAM S. BURROUGHS

William S. Burroughs is one of the greatest writers of our times. His talent has brought him fame, and along with it, many burdens. Daily, Burroughs is swamped with fan mail, unexpected visitors and interview requests. And if that wasn't enough to keep him occupied, strange rumors have begun circulating about him. Burroughs, who rarely grants interviews, speaks with Ron Whitehead in an attempt to counter the public's false speculation about him.

"His Swiftian vision of a processed, pre-packaged life, of a kind of electro-chemical totalitarianism, often evokes the black laughter of hilarious horror."
---Playboy

"Burroughs is the greatest satirical writer since Jonathan Swift."
---Jack Kerouac

"The only American writer possessed by genius."
---Norman Mailer

"Burroughs shakes the reader as a dog shakes a rat."
---Anthony Burgess

"An integrity beyond corruption...Burroughs convinces us he has seen things beyond description."
---John Updike

"One of the most dazzling magicians of our time."
---John Rechy, "The Ticket is Exploding"

"With suffering comes humility and with it in the end, wisdom."
---J. Swift

At 82, William Seward Burroughs II, El Hombre Invisible, Literary Outlaw, Commandeur de l'Ordre de Arts et des Lettres, is rapidly becoming the most respected, highly regarded writer in America, in the world.

"All at once I snapped my fingers a couple of times and laughed. Hellfire and damnation! I suddenly imagined I had discovered a new word! I sat up in bed, and said: It is not in the language, I have discovered it - Kuboaa. It has letters just like a real word, by sweet Jesus, man, you have discovered a word!...Kuboaa...of tremendous linguistic significance. The word stood out clearly in front of me in the dark."

Burroughs? No. Knut Hamsun. In 1890, with the publication of HUNGER, the first purely psychological novel (yes I'm ready to argue), Hamsun turned the literary world upside-down and spun it around. In 1959, 69 years after Hamsun's breakthrough, with the release of NAKED LUNCH, William S. Burroughs, explorer in the most real mythological sense, whose search for The Word has, does and will take him anywhere outside and inside himself, did what only a small handful of "literari" have achieved in the history of writing: He forever redirected the course of literature in a way that permanently altered language, culture and seeing.

So, what the hell is Old Bull Lee up to? Retired and enjoying good health, does he rest on his arse? No. He is busy working his arts off, dreaming, seeing, reading and representing new and old visions on paper, canvas, vinyl, tape, disk, CD-Rom, your brain and mine.

Dream long and dream hard enough
You will come to know
Dreaming can make it so
---William S. Burroughs

But rumors abound: He's kept tied to his bed and forced to use a chamber pot; he still takes heroin; he moved to central America (USA) because land was cheap and he knows it's about to become beachfront property since East and West coasts will be falling into oceans any day now; he's dead; he shoots obsessed, fatal-attraction European midnight visitors with a shotgun.

Come on people. Wake up. Sober down. William Burroughs is harassed day and night by folks from around the world showing up, without invitation, notice or warning, banging on doors and windows, camping in his yard, trying to get a glimpse of the legend.

The man is 82. Let's show respect for his privacy as we do for his work, as we would expect and demand given the good fortune of being in his position. He receives requests every day for interviews, visits, readings, recordings and films. He does what he can, and always, always in the friendliest manner. (And no, he hasn't shot or threatened anyone.)

William's latest books include "My Education: A Book of Dreams" and "Ghost of Chance." Recent audio work includes "Naked Lunch," "X-Files CD," plus, he is now in studio recording "Junky" and enjoying it so much he may go right into "Queer."

Two historic Burroughs events are taking place this summer. The Los Angeles County Museum of Art (you can contact them at 212-857-6522) is premiering the exhibition "Ports of Entry: William S. Burroughs and the Arts" on July 16 through October 6. The event, curated by Robert Sobieszek, is the first-ever retrospective surveying Burroughs' career, with 153 works, beginning with his 1960s and early 1970s photocollages, scrapbooks, and his collaborations with Brion Gysin on photomontage "cut-ups." The exhibition will also include Burroughs' later shotgun art and recent abstract painting, and will explore how his work has influenced today's cultural landscape, resulting in the absorption of his ideas and routines into newer art, advertising and current popular culture.

The second event is The New Orleans Voices Without Restraint INSOMNIACATHON 1996 at the Contemporary Arts Center and The

Howlin' Wolf Club, the largest Beat gathering of the year, where Mayor Mark Morial, James Grauerholz, Doug Brinkley, and others will speak with Burroughs over the phone.

Yes, the ticket is exploding. The walls of the literary world, the world of culture, are crumbling, and through the gaping holes strides the drawling wordslinger with an attitude, William Seward Burroughs II.

William S. Burroughs: Hello?

Ron Whitehead: William?

WSB: Yes.

Whitehead: Ron Whitehead.

WSB: Well, well, Ron Whitehead.

Whitehead: How the hell are you?

WSB: How what?

Whitehead: How are you?

WSB: Well, I'm fine, thank you.

Whitehead: As you recall, I produced your "Published in Heaven: Remembering Jack Kerouac poster and chapbook," plus I sent you my "Calling the Toads" poem & I'm right now producing the William S. Burroughs/Sonic Youth 7" vinyl recording for our audio series.

WSB: Oh, of course, yes, yes.

Whitehead: I just received letters from Rene in Amsterdam. He says that after my reading at the Meer den Woorden Festival in Goes,

Holland he started having dreams in which you and I taught him how to save the world. I'm forwarding the letters to you.

WSB: How old is he? I think I remember him. What does he look like?

Whitehead: Early 20s. Blond. Handsome. Friendly. Intelligent. Knows the history of the Beats inside out. He writes from a mental hospital in Amsterdam.

WSB: Hmm. Not sure. Perhaps.

Whitehead: Reason I'm calling is that Doug Brinkley has asked me to produce an event in New Orleans in August. It will be the largest Beat gathering of the year. RANT for the literary renaissance and The Majic Bus will present the event, called Voices Without Restraint: 48-Hour Non-Stop Music & Poetry INSOMNIACATHON 1996. As part of the event, we'll hold a City of New Orleans Presentation Ceremony, dedicating to you the historic marker which will be erected at your Algiers home, which was made famous by Jack Kerouac in "On the Road." And we'd like to have a live phone conversation with you during the presentation.

WSB: Why certainly. Yes, yes. I'm honored.

Whitehead: Good. Just a few questions.

WSB: Fine. Shoot.

Whitehead: Why did you decide to settle in Algiers, which at that time was home to various military bases, rather than in one of the traditional bohemian neighborhoods?

WSB: Yes. Because it was a hell of a lot cheaper. Real estate there was the cheapest. I got that house for $7,000 something.

Whitehead: Any memories of different New Orleans neighborhoods you visited, music, riding the ferry?

WSB: The Quarter, strange plays...Didn't get around too much.

Whitehead: The New Orleans Police have come under attack recently -- imagine that -- for corruption. A cop hired executioners to kill a woman who signed a brutality complaint against him. Louisiana police cars have "So no one will have to fear" inscribed on their sides. Do you have any observations about the New Orleans police, about the illegal search of your home there, or the firearms they confiscated?

WSB: No. They never laid a finger on me, as far as any brutality goes. They did lead me to believe that one of them was a federal agent when he wasn't. He was a city cop. So there was an illegal search. But I didn't know it at the time. The next day, I was arrested. There was someone with me I hardly knew. He was just introduced to me. He had one joint on him. He'd thrown out larger amounts but still had one, and they found it right away. Then the next day they went in and took my car and I never got it back, though I wasn't convicted of anything. See, they can confiscate your property even though you're not convicted of anything. And that's really scary sinister.

Whitehead: Both our political parties are looking like a bird with two right wings.

WSB: Exactly.

Whitehead: The police are gaining more powers daily as our personal freedoms are disappearing.

WSB: See, that's what I say. The whole drug war is nothing but a pretext to increase police power and personnel, and that, of course, is dead wrong. So many created imagined drug offenses.

Whitehead: New Orleans has North America's largest magic community. In recent years you've spoken bluntly about your interest in magic. In New Orleans did you encounter magic in any form?

WSB: No, I didn't.

Whitehead: There may be irony in having a literary marker commemorate your Algiers home, a place where you lived briefly, perhaps unhappily. Did you produce any writing there?

WSB: Oh yes, quite a bit. And I wouldn't say I was particularly unhappy there.

Whitehead: So it wasn't all that bad?

WSB: No, it wasn't. Not at all.

Whitehead: Jack Kerouac devoted a large section of "On the Road," on the New Orleans visit.

WSB: Oh well, Kerouac was writing fiction. What he did when he wrote about me...he made me out with Russian Countesses and Swiss accounts and other things I didn't have or didn't happen and so on. Yet...some truth, some fiction.

Whitehead: You have dramatically influenced music, literature, film, art, advertising and culture in general. Are you intrigued by that influence? How did you first become conscious of other people's perception of you as icon?

WSB: Well, slowly of course. Over time. Reading the paper, magazines, journals, that sort of thing.

Whitehead: The request for interviews becomes absurd after a while. This is the first and last one I intend to do. I feel uncomfortable in the position of interviewer.

WSB: Yes, it becomes absurd because interviewers generally ask the same questions, say the same things.

Whitehead: Recently you've been barraged with interview requests, especially in relation to the deaths of Timothy Leary and Jan Kerouac.

WSB: Yes, of course I knew Leary, but barely knew, didn't really know Jan. James knew her, was friends with her, but I didn't.

Whitehead: Hunter S. Thompson, who I like so much, is, like me, from Louisville and you're from just up the road in St. Louis. I recently visited Hunter at his home in Colorado. Hunter said he thought he was a pretty good shot until he went shooting with you.

WSB: I'll put it like this: Some days you're good and some you aren't.

Whitehead: You must have been good that day. Hunter was real impressed.

WSB: Well, he gave me a great pistol.

Whitehead: Like Hunter, some people would say that you're a Southern gentleman with a world literary reputation, but both you and Hunter have escaped the Southern-writer label. Any comments?

WSB: I escaped the label because I didn't and don't write about the South.

Whitehead: Do you have a personal favorite of your own readings? I know you've been in the studio recording "Junky."

WSB: No, I don't have any special favorite.

Whitehead: Other than Brion Gysin, is there anyone you miss the most?

WSB: When you get to be my age there are more and more people you have known that you miss. Brion, Antony Balch, Ian Summerville are ones I think of right away I was quite close to.

Whitehead: Diane di Prima is underrated, underappreciated in the world. Her autobiography will be released by Viking Penguin in April '97. I hope she'll finally receive credit that's long overdue.

WSB: Yes, I hope so too.

Whitehead: You've had much to say about Samuel Beckett. Beckett's mentor, James Joyce, was an anarchist who devoted his life work to undermining and deconstructing the dominant paradigm of patriarchy in government, religion, family and literature. I'm doing research asking The Beats what influence James Joyce had, if any, on their writing. How do you feel about Joyce?

WSB: Well he's great, a very great writer. Any modern writer is bound to be influenced by Joyce. Of course, by Beckett as well.

Whitehead: I had a long conversation with Allen Ginsberg about Bob Dylan. Allen talked about his personal feelings towards Dylan and also about Dylan's work. Allen said he felt like Dylan would be remembered long after The Beats and he added reasons why. This is a strong statement, especially coming from Allen Ginsberg. Do you have any comments on this?

WSB: No, I don't. Not in any cursory way. Of course, I've listened to and know his music and met him a couple of times, but I don't have any strong statements to make.

Whitehead: John Giorno is giving me an out-take from The Best of Bill CD box set he's producing. As part of White Fields Press' Published in Heaven series, I'm producing a 7" vinyl recording with you on one side and Sonic Youth on the other. Lee Renaldo has stopped by to visit you. How much are you able to keep up with music today?

WSB: Some much more than others. I've worked with and am very good friends with Patti Smith and Jim Carroll.

Whitehead: How do you feel about this historic marker?

WSB: Fine. Fine. It's an honor like the French Commandeur de l'Ordre des Arts et des Lettres. Commander of Arts and Letters. Commander of Arts and Letters.

originally published in LEO, Louisville Kentucky
BEAT SCENE, England
TRIBE, New Orleans Louisiana

CALLING THE TOADS

                    Hummm
Hummm
                    Hummm
                Hummm
           Hummm
        Hummm
Hummm
  Hummm
Calling the toads
Calling the toads
We shall come rejoicing
Calling the toads

      one step out the door off the step
      goin down swingin
      in a peyote amphetamine benzedrine
      dream
      I'm five years old I am the messenger holdin
      William Burroughs' Bill Burroughs'
      Old Bull Lee's hand
      holdin Bill's hand on some lonely
      godforsakinuppermiddleclassSt.Louisstreet
      and we're hummin we're hummin
      we're hummin in tones
      we're hummin in tones
      callin the toads
      oh yeah we're callin the toads
      Bill's eyes twinklin glitterin
      a devilish grin crackin the corners
      of his mouth and I'm lookin him
      right smack in the eyes
      deep in the eyes I'm readin
      his heroined heart yes I'm readin his old heart
      but it ain't the story I expected
      as we move this way and that

raisin and lowerin out heads our voices
callin the toads
and here they come
marchin high and low from
under the steps from under
the shrooms of the front yard
from round the corner of the house
fallin from the trees
rainin down here come the toads
all sizes and shapes all swingin
and swayin and dancin that
magic Burroughs Beat
yes here come the toads singin
and swayin and swingin their hips
now standin all round us
hundreds thousands of toads
eyes bulgin tongues stickin out   hard
dancin a strange happy vulgar rhythmed
dance for Burroughs and me
yes Burroughs yes Burroughs
yes Burroughs I see his heart
and I know his secret
a secret no one has discovered
til now but I'll never tell
never reveal as I witness
this sacred scene this holy ceremony
this gathering
this universal song and dance
I witness through the eyes the heart
of William S. Burroughs
King of the Toads

          Calling the toads
          Calling the toads
            We shall come rejoicing
Calling the toads   Hummmm

5
i refuse

Sarah & Ron, The C-Note, New York City 2004, photo by Jeremy Hogan

i refuse

part 1:

i refuse

i refuse to wear a seatbelt
i refuse to take a breathalyzer
i refuse to take a mandatory drug test
i refuse to take a mandatory polygraph
i refuse to take a mandatory anything

i refuse

i refuse to cut my hair
i refuse to shave my beard
i refuse to wear underwear
i refuse to go to the derby

i refuse

i refuse background credit checks in order to get a job
i refuse background medical checks in order to get a job
i refuse medical exams in order to get a job

i refuse

i refuse to bow down to any government
i refuse to bow down to any religion
i refuse to bow down to any corporation
i refuse to bow down to any military
i refuse to bow down to any secret court

i refuse to bow down to any dogma

i refuse

i refuse to accept or adhere to meaningless laws
i refuse to fight wars for despots for tyrants for powermongers
i refuse to fight wars

i refuse

i refuse to hurt anyone

i refuse

i refuse to stop drinking red wine
i refuse to stop smoking marijuana
i refuse to stop taking mescaline and peyote

i refuse

i refuse to stop living my non-violent warrior life on my own terms
i refuse to bow down to anyone or anything

i refuse
i refuse
i refuse
i refuse to kiss anybody's ass except Sarah's
i refuse to kiss ass
i refuse to do anything big brother asks me to do
i refuse big brother

i refuse

i refuse to be spanked by anyone but Sarah

i refuse

i refuse to wear pink tights or panties or any other women's clothes
    cept maybe a woman's cowboy hat every now and then
    but you go ahead and wear whatever you want to wear

i refuse to tell anyone what to do
   unless they're hurting someone
   then i'll do all i can to stop them
i refuse to be a disciplinarian or an authoritarian

i refuse

i refuse to be a member of the status quo
i refuse to live in the suburbs
i refuse to sleep too much
i refuse to be a zombie
i refuse to submit to anyone or anything

i refuse

i refuse to go to church
i refuse to have anything to do with a church or an undertaker
i refuse to believe anything you ask or tell me to believe
i refuse to tell a lie
i refuse to allow you to bring me down

i refuse marriage
i refuse divorce
i refuse

i refuse
i refuse
i refuse

i refuse to hurt anyone or anything
i refuse to hurt Mother Earth
i refuse to hurt my family friends allies guides angels
i refuse to hurt my enemies

i refuse

i refuse to be angry
i refuse to hate
i refuse to follow any path but the path of love

i refuse

i refuse
i refuse
i refuse

This Is a Metaphysical Poem

1) (Sock) Monkeys Rule The World
2) Attempting The Impossible
3) THE THIRD KINGDOM: Synthesis of Irreconcilable Differences
4) Juxtaposition of Apparently Ambiguous Elements
5) 4th Person Singular: Bridge Over Troubled Water
6) She Came, Finally!
7) MYSTERIUM TREMENDUM: The Numinous Guerrilla Ensemble
8) This Is A Metaphysical Poem
9) And The Wind Cried
10) You Know Nothing (he said simultaneously to himself and the entire world)
11) he makes 6-foot womanly vases and paints them naked with bird and animal heads
12) to live in a hut and drift to sleep warmed by the fading wolf song
13) Moving Mystery Theatre

A Prayer

after Burroughs

> like a bird on a wire
> like a drunk in the midnight choir
> I have tried all my life
> to be free
> --Leonard Cohen

thanks for the wild turkey and the half pound of ground round
destined to be shit out through wholesome usa guts

thanks for a continent a world to despoil and poison
thanks for Native Americans Afghanis and Iraqis to provide
a modicum of challenge danger and entertainment

thanks for vast herds of bison to kill and skin
leaving the carcasses to rot thanks for bounties
on wolves bears and coyotes thanks for the usa dream

to vulgarize to falsify until the bare lies shine through
thanks for the kkk for neo-nazis and for a new
secret fear based government that is dismantling

our Constitution our Bill of Rights and increasing
censorship thanks for nigger-killin lawmen feelin
their notches thanks for decent church-goin men

and women with their mean pinched bitter evil
faces who don't understand that Jesus never
killed nobody who don't understand that there's

only One Commandment not 10 who don't understand
thanks for Kill a Queer for Christ Kill and Eat a Vegan
bumper stickers thanks for laboratory AIDS thanks

for Prohibition and the bogus War On Drugs thanks
for a country where nobody's allowed to mind
their own business thanks for a nation of snitches

thanks for filling the prisons for building new prisons
and filling them too so corporations can continue
to have slave labor Yes Thanks for all the memories

thanks for the last and greatest betrayal of
the last and greatest of human dreams

        --with Special Thanks to my friend William S. Burroughs

Dreams Memories Visions
for Ron Whitehead

by Gui Sedley Stuart

dust travelin through time in an hourglass
of dreams memories and visions that are

encapsulated in the shifting tides of perception
spinning us out of the will out to the four

corners like seeds that have been blown
out of the hand of the creator and spread

out across the earth by the wind until some
of them dig in and grow roots in Kentucky

somewhere on the fringe of time in time
and out of time all the time in this time

my beard long my neck high my head bent
into a microphone as the rivers of my soul

pour out of my mouth as the hills of my
heritage roll out of me like the hills of

Kentucky as the force of my spirit churns
its way out of my heart and fills the room

with energy fills the room with the charisma
of my soul in the passion of my heart where

all the lakes form and the rivers start where
the fire continues to burn on an island in a

body in a battle ground called Kentucky
and my wife plays and sings next to me

and her voice brings the audience to tears
it is the blues in bluegrass come a callin

at the twilight night that comes moanin
and longin before the dawn breaks and

the sun opens up on the remnants of
yesteryear on the rubble of yesterday and

The Viking Hillbilly Apocalypse Revue
transcends the audience and transforms

the night into a happy forlorn beauty that's
been almost forgotten too many times

pushed aside for insignificant things that
don't matter in the long run that don't matter

in the beat of your heart or the bottled up
love in your soul and the night is alive

now I am alive in the night I conjure up
the spirits and they perform with us and

they're all around us and they make us
strong and I am ancient like the spirits

I've been dust before and will be dust
again and right now the dust of my

forefathers sweeps through me there
are spirits in that dust boy that dust

sweeps through time boy like sand
sifting through an hourglass and the

life of the ancients the life of the fire
eternal is in that dust and the breezes

of Kentucky blow it into me and you
as we journey through the trials and trails

of our lives that fire rekindles and
reincarnates our souls and I come

to you in Kentucky from Kentucky
out of Kentucky in the world and

sometimes out of the world and out
of the body and always inside the

universe the universe of verse and
I try and make my body a lantern

illuminating the pathway the trail
which we all must traverse like a guide

a guide a spirit a spirit guide to glide
ahead and study the terrain with my

brain with my heart with my window
eyes to try and capture a glimpse and

a little bit of wisdom from all from the
all seeing eye that watches over the

universe and I aim to keep that fire alive
and to spread it wherever I can wherever

I go wherever I am cause the fire is life
and the drum of our hearts beats to it

for eternity and the passion of our souls
lives in its flame don't live in vain

GIMME BACK MY WIG
The Hound Dog Taylor Hunter S. Thompson Blues

Gimme Back My Wig
I Got The Hound Dog Taylor Hunter S. Thompson
Gimme Back My Wig
I Gotta Get Out Of This Town   Blues

Gimme Back My Wig
cause I'm thumbin a ride after midnight on
The Hound Dog Taylor Alligator
New Orleans Memphis Chicago 61 Blues Highway yes
I gotta get out of this town fore somebody does me in

Gimme Back My Wig
the blonde crew cut is the only one that'll work now
cause it's already late
maybe too late in these last days final hours of this Rush
Limbaugh Newt Gingrich Pat Buchanan Jesse
Helms George Bush Ronald Reagan Richard
Nixon Joseph McCarthy J. Edgar Hoover
Cheney Ashcroft Rumsfield Rove Bush Jr
new age government this Pat Robertson
Jerry Falwell cult ☐merican☐ coalition
moral majority ☐merican renaissance
KKK neonazi militiaman takeover of
America

the Land of the Free Home of the Brave
we Killed the Indians why not the
Decadent Poets Artists Musicians
Blacks Jews Hispanics Asians
Muslims HomoLesbians Beat
Generation X Smart Women

Outsiders the Sad Downtrodden
Stepped on Walked on
Kicked and Killed
all the morally
depraved

yes please Gimme Back My Wig
I don't think the red Afro gonna work need that
skinhead look tonight slippin
left to right and over the fence outta this hellhole backstreet
underground alley I been crowded into by
American
brownshirtarmbandschoolyardBullyThugs

Gimme Back My Wig
I'm climbing out the back window paint brushes and pens
old canvases crumpled papers peanut butter sandwich
hanging from my back all my possessions as The Swat
Team breaks down the front door cause I'm behind
on my rent and The Land Lord come
to pay me a visit

yes I'm evicted convicted of being on the wrong side
and I'm convinced that this new state is taxation
without representation and I've watched this
new state force the 1st Amendment to
disappear and I've experienced the
protection of this new omnipotent
police state of by and for
the rich

yes I say it's high time
to put on my wig
and finally
say
goodbye

cause I Got a Lethal Dose of
The Hound Dog Taylor Hunter S. Thompson
Gimme Back My Wig
I Gotta Get Out Of This Town Blues

I Found Myself in Emptiness

I found myself in emptiness, terror
wrapped round my heart a wall of fear, panic
I found myself in emptiness, panic
waking up in fear suffering was all
waking up in fear suffering was all
I found myself in emptiness, panic
wrapped round my heart a wall of fear, panic
I found myself in emptiness, terror

the guide and I in silence sat, seeing
I found myself in emptiness, silent
the guide and I in silence sat, waiting
I found myself in emptiness, silent
the guide and I in silence sat, listening
I found myself in emptiness, silent

virtual photons we: zero signature

virtual photons we
dark matter

objects in space
seen and unseen

shadow waves
of energy echoes

birthing dna
from galactic center

emanates birthing
brain cells bodies

energy beings we
do not die we shadow

waves emanate in
through beyond

time and space
we are we are we are

multi dimensional
eternal one all of us

us is one
virtual photons

swimming sailing
through dark matter

objects in space
shadow waves of

clothed and naked
energy echoes birthing

dna in kentucky in
greece on appalachian

mountains in new york city
on portuguese beaches

sparrows eating bread
crumbs on the balcony

lovers in the tree house
ra energy emanate imminent

spiraling third fourth
dimensions and beyond

invisible dust
of potential stars

go beyond go beyond
go beyond go virtual

photons we go

I Will Not Bow Down: global version

"I, Chief Arvol Looking Horse, of the Lakota, Dakota, and Nakota Nation, ask you to understand an indigenous perspective on what has happened in America, what we call 'Turtle Island.' My words seek to unite the global community through a message from our sacred ceremonies to unite spiritually, each in our own ways of beliefs in the Creator.

We have been warned from Ancient Prophecies of these times we live in today, but have also been given a very important message about a solution to turn these terrible times around.

To understand the depth of this message you must recognize the importance of Sacred Sites and realize the interconnectedness of what is happening today, in reflection of the continued massacres that are occurring on other lands and our own Americas.

I have been learning about these important issues since the age of 12, upon receiving the Sacred White Buffalo Calf Pipe Bundle and its teachings. Our people have striven to protect Sacred Sites from the beginning of time. These places have been violated for centuries and have brought us to the predicament that we are in at the global level.

Look around you. Our Mother Earth is very ill from these violations, and we are on the brink of destroying the possibility of a healthy and nurturing survival for generations to come, our children's children."
 --Chief Arvol Looking Horse, Chief of The Great Sioux Nation

I will not bow down

I will not bow down
to your Government
   to your Religion

I Will Not Bow Down
   to your Materialism
   to your International Corporations
   to your Religious Shrines
      your Stock Markets
      your Shopping Malls

I Will Not Bow Down
   to your Coal Mines
   to your Oil Refineries
   to your Nuclear Plants

I Will Not go crawling down the deep shafts at midnight

I Will Not Bow Down
   to your invasion of privacy
   to your moral absolutes
      your religious political might

I Will Not Bow Down
   to your Assassins
      the International Corporate Police State
      the World Trade Organization
      your Killing Murdering Machines

I Will Not Bow Down
   to your Bureaucracies
   to your Schools
   to your attempt to make me the model citizen
      of your State of your Church

I Will Not Bow Down
   to your Fear-Based Hissstory
      of Lies
   to your Secrets
      in the Best Interest of

      to protect
      the People

I Pledge Allegiance
    to those who were here before you
    to those who will be here after you are gone

I Pledge Allegiance
    to the woman I love

I Pledge Allegiance
    to my children to my grandchildren
            to all my children to come

I Pledge Allegiance
    to my family friends and allies
    to my guides and angels
        seen and unseen

I Pledge Allegiance
    to poetry to music to art
    to the global literary renaissance
    to the global arts community

I Pledge Allegiance to the Beat to the Outsider

I Pledge Allegiance to meditation to stillness
    to magic to beautiful mysticism to ecstasy
    to AH and AHA
    to the Big Bang Epiphany
    to altered states of consciousness

I Pledge Allegiance
    to seeing
        into the occult the unknown
    to seeing

    into every day into the ordinary
      and being amazed

I Pledge Allegiance to the Sacred and the Profane
    to gnostical turpitude

I Pledge Allegiance to my physical body
    and to the knowledge that I am more than
      my physical body

I Pledge Allegiance to seeing more than
    the physical world and to those
    of higher frequency vibration
    and consciousness

I Pledge Allegiance to passing through
      the Sacred Fire
    to entering the upper chamber of the golden pyramid
    to levitating over the open sarcophagus
    to out of body experience

I Pledge Allegiance to hard work

I Pledge Allegiance to labor unions

I Pledge Allegiance to honesty

I Pledge Allegiance to red wine

I Pledge Allegiance to the hottest sex
    and to gentle affection

I Pledge Allegiance to fractal geometry
      the geometry of clouds and coastlines
    to 2x2 equaling 5

I Pledge Allegiance to Failure
   to failing as no other dare fail

I Pledge Allegiance to taking risks
   to holy daring
   to accepting responsibility for my own actions
   to helping my neighbors

I Pledge Allegiance to not achieving
   the International Corporate Dream of Success

I Pledge Allegiance to trees to green grass
   to brown earth to wildflowers of every color
   to wilderness to turquoise indigenous skies
     to native peoples everywhere
     to dolphins and whales
     to rivers lakes and seas
     to healing the earth

I Pledge Allegiance to the Holy Spirit
   to the Word and to Silence

I Pledge Allegiance to Dreams

I Pledge Allegiance to Birth to the Journey and to Death

I Pledge Allegiance to No Mas to I Am No More

I Pledge Allegiance
   to Candor to Sincerity to Laughter to Irony

I Pledge Allegiance to Passion to Compassion
   to Empathy and to Helping Those in Need

I Pledge Allegiance to Resurrection of the Heart

I Pledge Allegiance to GOing Beyond Beyond Beyond

NO
I Will Not Bow Down

6
Creative Marriage

Ron proposed to Sarah, Montgomery, Alabama 2003, photo by Valerie Downes

if the trials and tribulations of today
don't make us wiser tomorrow
then we remain suffering fools

I will destroy my enemies
by making them my friends

blue skies   red wine
backroads   railroads
spring

Creative Marriage

There are many ways many paths open to us. But truth is actually a pathless land. Each of us must decide where to step, what path or what wilderness to wander on or through, as we seek meaning, as we discover who we are. There is nothing more important for each of you than to discover, step by step, who you are. The words gnothi seauton, know thyself, were inscribed over the doorway the entranceway to the temple of Apollo, high on the mountainside, high above the Gulf of Corinth, in ancient Greece, greeting all neophytes, all who came to devote the remainder of their lives in search of truth. How can you know another, your significant other, your lover, your best friend, your husband, your wife, unless until you know yourself. And knowing yourself is a lifelong process. And even when you reach the end of your life you will have only arrived at the beginning. The process of self-growth is perpetual, it is eternal.

So let go of judging, of trying to change your lover, or anyone else. Accept them as they are. Encourage them to find their own dream and live it. Nurture them with love. But do not criticize or condemn, do not judge. There is no judgment. There is only love.

Discover who you are. Learn to stand on your own two feet. The best government is the government of individual responsibility. Be responsible for yourself, for your own actions. Learn to love and support yourself. You are not responsible for anyone else. But nurture and help your lover, and your neighbors, especially those who can't help themselves: children, the elderly, the sick. Be a good neighbor.

Modern day prophet, greatest psychic of all time, Sunday school teacher all his life, Kentucky farmboy, grew up outside Hopkinsville, Edgar Cayce said lightning is the closest we can come to knowing God in nature. One certain true way to establish God's kingdom on earth is by connecting with the light, the lightning light, the God Light within each of us. We are all fools. But simultaneously we are all wise.

Choose daily to realize your wisdom your true self buried in your heart in your soul in your innermost being. Remember the quiet pure true inner sanctuary of your own being. Rise early, pray and meditate. A few minutes is all it takes. Meditation is simply being still and listening. Listening is the greatest art of all. Pray prayers of thanks for the blessed gift of life of love. Pray then Listen. We ask often. But we seldom, if ever, listen. Listen to your intuition to your heart and soul. Listen to The Great Spirit to God. Open yourself, invite the Holy Spirit to dwell to move in and through you always. Be Light and Love. Be true to Yourself, to your own spirit and soul. Find your dream. Build a bridge from where you are to where you want to be. Take one step at a time. Develop your will. Go beyond. By going further than you ever thought you could go you will develop your will. With a strong will you will achieve accomplish more than you ever dreamed was possible.

By choosing to be guided by your heart and soul, by honoring yourself, you will be able to love and accept each other as you are. By continually striving to grow you will allow your lover the same freedom. To Grow.

Embrace light, live love. Practice daily. Project your light and love into the world. The mists the fog will be dispelled. Do not look to others to do this work for you. Do not judge them when they don't. Do it yourself, project light and love from yourself into the world. Ask for nothing. Be content. Do not want what is not yours. Be satisfied. Do not look up to or down at anyone. Recognize that we are all in this together.

Know that the creative imagination is the doorway to spiritual realms. The creative imagination provides salvation from the mundane, from death in life. You are two of the most creative, light-filled, and loving people I have ever known. Keep your creative flames burning.

Forgiveness is amazing grace. It is central. Learn to forgive yourself thereby enabling forgiveness of others. Forgiveness is a learned process. Learn to forgive. Practice Forgiveness.

Be honest. Always. With yourself then with everyone. Be honest.

Communicate. Be open and honest with each other, with everyone. Have no secrets. Be an open book. With nothing to hide you will breathe easier. You will know Peace and Happiness.

And I close with a Blessing of the Apaches:

Now you will feel no rain, for each of you will be shelter for the other.
Now you will feel no cold, for each of you will be warmth to the other.
Now there will be no loneliness, for each of you will be companion to the other.
Now you are two persons, but there is only one life before you.
May beauty surround you both in the journey ahead and through all the years.
May happiness be your companion and your days together be good and long upon the earth.

7
The Hunter S. Thompson Blastoff is Decadent and Depraved

Hunter S. Thompson & Ron Whitehead playing with guns & fire, Colorado, USA [A.H.A.]

Hunter S. Thompson & Ron playing with guns & fire
Owl Farm, Woody Creek, Colorado, 1995

en route to Owl Farm

borrowed car
borrowed time
no insurance

Dr. Hunter Shaman Thompson is dead
a tribute

My friend and hero Hunter S. Thompson is dead. I followed his life and work from the release of HELL'S ANGELS till now. I will continue to follow it. I sold Hunter's books I sold the first ROLLING STONE magazines in the underground bookstore, For Madmen Only, and in the headshop, The Store, Gene Williams and I operated on South Limestone in Lexington Kentucky. I never dreamed I'd eventually work with Hunter and with members of The Beat Generation: Allen Ginsberg, William S. Burroughs, Herbert Huncke, Gregory Corso, Lawrence Ferlinghetti, David Amram, Diane di Prima, Amiri Baraka, and others. Their works changed my life. Dreams do come true.

Hunter shot himself. He is gone. He died in his kitchen in his cabin at Owl Farm Woody Creek Colorado. I read his Nixon obituary, "He Was A Crook," and other works to him in that kitchen. I took my children to visit him. He loved young people. He loved his family. I drank and did drugs with him. We watched basketball. One night, years ago, in early May my son Nathanial and I arrived, driving 24 hours non-stop from Kentucky, just in time to watch the NBA playoffs with Hunter. Don Johnson called several times wanting us to come over. Kentuckian Rex Chapman was playing for the Phoenix Suns. The Suns were down by nine points with one minute to go in the game. I looked at Hunter and said I'll bet you that Rex will hit three threes and tie the game, that the Suns will win by one point in three overtimes. Hunter looked at me and laughed. Rex hit three threes and tied the game. But Phoenix lost in three overtimes, by one point. I got damn close. Hunter paid closer attention to me after that. We talked about life about our families about literature. Hunter was a good kind man. He was full of life. He was tough. He was a real human being. He was spirit, holy spirit, no matter what anyone says.

I had the honor of producing, with the help of Douglas Brinkley and many young people and friends, The Hunter S. Thompson Tribute at Memorial Auditorium on 4th Street in Louisville Kentucky in

December 1996. We had a sold out standing room audience of over 2,000. I brought in Hunter, his Mom Virginia, his son Juan, The Sheriff of Pitkin County, Johnny Depp, Warren Zevon, David Amram, Douglas Brinkley, Roxanne Pulitzer, Harvey Sloane, Susi Wood & a bluegrass band, and many more. The Mayor gave Hunter the keys to the city. The Governor named Hunter, Johnny, Warren, David, Doug, and me Kentucky Colonels. Thank You J.B. and Steve Wilson for working with the Governor to make us Kentucky Colonels. The Hunter S. Thompson Tribute was a spectacular event. In March 2005 Sarah and I produced a standing room only Hunter Tribute at The Rudyard Kipling. Another awesome evening with numberous heartfilled tearstained tributes to Hunter.

Hunter is one of America's one of the world's greatest writers. He stands shoulder to shoulder with Mark Twain, John Steinbeck, Jack Kerouac, William S. Burroughs, all five America's Best prose writers, bar none.

Jonathan Swift, George Orwell, William S. Burroughs, and Hunter S. Thompson are literary giants, visionaries who have much in common.

People continue to say that there will be no audience for Thompson's work, that no one will understand or care. Yet as I travel across America across the world working with young people, of all ages, I witness a movement, amongst young people, away from the constraints of non-democratic puritan totalitarian cultures. I see a new generation that recognizes the lies of the power elite, a generation that is turning to the freethinkers the freedom fighters of the 50s and 60s, recognizing honoring them as mentors.

Art is a kind of innate drive that seizes a human being and makes her or him its instrument. The artist is not simply a person acting freely, in pursuit of a merely private end, but one who allows art to realize its purposes through her or his person. Artists have moods, free will, personal aims, but as artists they are bearers of a collective humanity, carrying and shaping the common unconscious life of the species.

I have heard more than once that Hunter S. Thompson is a madman. That oh look at what he could have done if he lived a more sane life. Nobel Prize winner Elie Wiesel, pre-eminent Jewish author, recipient of the Nobel Peace Prize, in THE TOWN BEYOND THE WALL, says: "Mad Moishe, the fat man who cries when he sings and laughs when he is silent...Moishe - I speak of the real Moishe, the one who hides behind the madman - is a great man. He is far-seeing. He sees worlds that remain inaccessible to us. His madness is only a wall, erected to protect us- us: to see what Moishe's bloodshot eyes see would be dangerous." In Jewish mysticism the prophet often bears the facade of madness. Hunter S. Thompson stands in direct lineage to the great writers and prophets. And as with the prophets of old, the message may be too painful for the masses to tolerate, to hear, to bear. They may, and usually do, condemn, even kill, the messenger. Hunter stood as long as he could. He fought a valiant fight. He was a brave yet sensitive soul. He was a sacred shaman warrior. He saw. He felt. He recorded his visions. He took alcohol and drugs to ease the pain generated by what he saw what he felt. He lived on his own terms. He died on his own terms. Did the masses kill Hunter? Did he kill himself? He found the courage to stand up against the power mongers and the masses. At least thirteen times he should have died but, miraculously, didn't. He chose to take his own life. He completed the work he came to do. His Termination Date arrived. He came, he saw, he conquered, he departed.

If life is a dream, as some suggest, sometimes beautiful sometimes desperate, then Hunter's work is the terrible saga of the ending of time for The American Dream. With its action set at the heart of darkness of American materialist culture, with war as perpetual background, playing on the television, Hunter S. Thompson, like the prophets of old, shows how we, through greed and powerlust, have already gone over the edge. As Jack Kerouac, through his brilliant oeuvre, breathed hope into international youth culture Thompson shows how the ruling power-elite is not about to share what it controls with idealists yearning for a world of peace love and understanding.

We must look beyond the life of the artist to the work the body of work itself. That is the measure of success. Like those who have re-examined Orwell's 1984 to find a multi-layered literary masterpiece, we must look deep into Thompson's work and find the deep multi-layered messages. His books, especially the early ones and his letters, are literary masterpieces equal to the best writing ever produced.

Knowledge, from the inception of Modernism, and through post-modernism and chaos to The Ocean of Consciousness, is reorganized, redefined through Literature, Art, Music, and Film. The genres are changing, the canons are exploding, as is culture. The mythopoetics, the privileged sense of sight, of modern, contemporary, avant-garde cutting edge Nabi poets, musicians, artists, filmmakers are examples of art forms of a society, a culture, a civilization, a world, in which humanity lives, not securely in cities nor innocently in the country, but on the apocalyptic, simultaneous edge of a new realm of being and understanding. The mythopoet, female and male, the shaman, Hunter S. Thompson returns to the role of prophet-seer by creating myths that resonate in the minds of readers, myths that speak with the authority of the ancient myths, myths that are gifts from the shadow.

The Hunter S. Thompson Blastoff is Decadent and Depraved

by Ron Whitehead and Sarah Elizabeth

~~I've rarely seen such security. All Friday and Saturday security guards, dressed in black, lined the road from Highway 82 outside Aspen, down across Woody Creek all along Woody Creek Road for miles on each side of Hunter's Owl Farm. Plus security was arm to arm surrounding the property. We drove from The Woody Creek Tavern to Owl Farm stopping for Sarah to take a photo of me at the Gonzoed mailbox with Woody Creek Road sign. To our astonishment a huge black SUV drove up to us and stopped. It had GONZO POLICE signs on both sides. It was filled with sneering demon-faced thugs. Sarah had already taken the photo so we walked back to our car. The Gonzo Police drove away. I was astonished. Gonzo Police?! Is this possible? Having Gonzo Police patrol a Hunter Thompson party is like me having Poetry Police patrol one of my 48-hour non-stop music and poetry Insomniacathons. It's beyond absurd. It's frightening! The negative energies my increasingly raw nerves were picking up were taking me to a bad bad place.~~

Not Better Than Sex

Douglas Brinkley sent me the invitation, via email and phone, for the wake, a celebration of Hunter S. Thompson's life and work, an event that would culminate in the blasting of his ashes from a cannon mounted at the top of a monument of his Gonzo fist, a 15-story 153-foot tower, higher than the Statue of Liberty, modeled after Hunter's logo: clenched fist, holding a peyote button, two thumbs, all rising from the hilt of a dagger. Family and friends were being invited. Fellow Kentuckian, and all round nice guy, Johnny Depp, now living in France, was producing the event paying $2.5 million out of his own pocket. A few rich and famous friends of Hunter would be in attendance. Music would be provided by Hunter's friends Lyle Lovett, The Nitty Gritty Dirt Band, and David Amram. Sarah might sing "My Old Kentucky Home," a Hunter favorite. It would all take place on Hunter's Owl Farm, Woody Creek, near Aspen, in the heart of Colorado.

But things changed. Word got out about the event. The press and the gliterrati picked up on it. Suddenly large sums were being offered, under the table, to get an invite. A Hollywood firm was hired to handle everything, including the invitations. Brinkley bowed out as Gate Keeper. David Amram told us not to go that it was out of control, crazy, pure madness. We decided to stay home. We were too busy to get jerked around. We had better things to do. Plus Sarah and I weren't really in a financial position to pay the $600 we guestimated it would cost to make the trip.

In December 1996 I produced The Official Hunter S. Thompson Tribute at Memorial Auditorium in Hunter's hometown of Louisville, Kentucky. I brought in Johnny Depp, Warren Zevon, Roxanne Pulitzer, Douglas Brinkley, David Amram, Harvey Sloane, Hunter's mom Virginia, his son Juan, The Sheriff of Pitkin County (Hunter's bodyguard), and many others including some of Hunter's childhood friends. It was an amazing event. The energy was sky high. Electricity filled the over 2,000 standing room only crowd. A & E filmed it as did Hollywood filmmaker Wayne Ewing who had just finished filming The Eagles' Last Tour. The event was a huge success. The problem was that one week before the event the University of Louisville, fearful of negative publicity, withdrew their sponsorship. The event cost $80,000, a small sum compared to the $2.5 million Johnny paid to produce the Blastoff. We earned $30,000 from ticket and merchandise sales. I got stuck with the $50,000 balance to pay out of my pocket. A $30,000 balance remains. Sarah and I are still paying on it. Of the over 1,000 music and poetry events I produced all over Europe and the USA, in the past 15 years, this was the biggest loser. On all but five I broke even, lost a little, or made a little. When I made a little the extra money went into the next creative project.

Wayne Ewing filmed the 1996 Hunter Tribute so it could be included in his newly released cinema verite documentary *Breakfast With Hunter*. The film is brilliant. Wayne used a great deal of footage from the Hunter Tribute I produced. At the 1996 Tribute Wayne agreed, on a handshake, to send me copies of both his film of the '96 Tribute and the final product, *Breakfast With Hunter*. After the '96 Tribute I talked with Hunter and Wayne about the $50,000 loss. I never heard from Wayne again. Sarah and I paid $49 to order Wayne's new documentary from his website. I was glad Wayne used so much footage from my Hunter Tribute. But I was furious that he credited the University of Louisville for producing the event. I wrote Wayne an angry email asking that credits be changed and that he send us copies of the DVD. While in Colorado for Hunter's Blastoff I got word, from various sources, that Hunter's beautiful wife Anita and his wonderful son Juan had been told that I was going to file a lawsuit against Hunter's Estate. A lie. Before leaving Colorado I wrote them a letter to set straight the lies of the grapevine.

Yes at the last minute Sarah and I decided to go. David Amram, despite his warnings to us, decided to go so by God we did too. Besides, we wanted the adventure. Plus we realized that in nearly two years of being married we hadn't taken a honeymoon trip. All our trips and tours to Europe and across America had been to perform, for me to read my poems and stories and for Sarah to sing her songs. We decided that regardless of what happened at the Hunter Blastoff that we were going to have a romantic interlude in the midst of our workaholic writing and performing schedule.

But how to get to Colorado?! Our 1988 Toyota pickup, Sarah's dad's old work truck, has 230,000 miles on it. It's dependable but could it climb the Rocky Mountains? Out of the blue our friend Andy Cook, who has toured with us for years, gave us his 1989 Nissan pickup which only has 90,000 miles on it. What a surprise! We didn't know if our new/used Nissan would make it but we decided to find out. Then an hour before departure my sister Robin called and asked if she could borrow Sarah's '88 open bed truck to move her daughter, my niece, Heidi, back to Eastern Kentucky University for her final semester. Robin said in exchange we could drive her Mitsubishi sports car to Colorado. Are you kidding me?! We were as excited as kids at Christmas. Now, finally, we were on our way.

We drove 24 hours non-stop. We left Thursday, noon. I called and left messages with Anita and Juan Thompson to let them know we were on our way. All night, through Kansas, wild lightning storms covered the terrain in front of us and to our right. But to our left and behind us the sky was clear and the full moon shone through our open moonroof and brightened the high plains. Sarah and I had breakthrough conversations all night. We were ecstatic, excited, on cloud nine discussing our love, our work, our family, our lives together. We were happy to be on another adventure, our first since our 19 day, 14 county, 325 mile western Kentucky hike back in May. We discussed the book we're writing about the hike.

At daybreak we began our climb from Pike's Peak taking backroads crossing the heart of Colorado. We stopped at Independence Pass, the highest and most beautiful point in Colorado, on our way to Aspen.

I was in trouble. In 2003, in the days leading up to Bush's Iraq invasion, while on The War Poets Tour of Iceland, Scotland, and England, with Frank Messina, Andy Cook, and Sarah, after our first show at the Museum of Modern Art in Reykjavik I had two lung aneurisms. In 2004, while on The Viking Hillbilly Apocalypse Revue's coast to coast USA Tour I had a series of mild heart attacks. I no longer do well at high altitude. The fatigue of the long non-stop drive added to the fatigue of overworking plus now the high altitude was taking its toll. It started with my heart, chest pains, then lungs, struggle to breathe plus dizziness, then kidneys, frequent and profuse urination plus dehydration, then nerves, hyper-sensitivity to positive and negative vibrations from people and environment. But I've been through all this before. Sarah and I, like Hunter, are both road warriors. I refused to let my pain diminish the excitement of the adventure.

We arrived at Headquarters, The Wildwood Lodge in Snowmass Village, closer to Woody Creek and Hunter's Owl Farm than Aspen and less expensive. We took a two-hour nap, showered then made our way to The Woody Creek Tavern, Hunter's main hangout, for a meal, to begin paying final Tribute to Hunter, and to visit with the pilgrims who had hiked, hitchhiked, and driven Gonzoed vehicles from every corner of America for the same reason we had, to pay Tribute to their hero, fallen by his own hand, the Creator and King of Gonzo, Dr. Hunter S. Thompson. And, we discovered, they were all going to try and break into The Big Party.

I come from a long line of farmers, coal miners, holy roller preachers, musicians, storytellers, and strong women. Sarah comes from a long line of farmers, mechanics, coal miners, and strong Cherokee women. The people we met at The Woody Creek Tavern were blue collar working class, poor, downtrodden, stubborn, strong-willed, independent, resistant individuals who will not be told, by church or state or anyone else, how to live their lives. They are American dissidents. Dissidence is not un-American. Our country was born of dissidence. We dissented against our parent, England, went our own way and formed a new country, the USA. Many people died in the process. We fought for the right the freedom to dissent, the freedom to agree or disagree with our government, with anyone, and not be punished for dissenting. *The Declaration of Independence, The Constitution,* and *The Bill of Rights* are the most important political documents ever conceived, written, and made into law. The pilgrims at The Woody Creek Tavern understood all this. They live their lives accordingly regardless of the consequences. So did Hunter S. Thompson. And Hunter went a step further. He expressed his dissent in his life and his writing. His books became best sellers. Hunter is popular all over the world. He was bold, courageous, outrageous in ways many people are fearful of. But even more admire Hunter for having the courage to be a beacon of what it means to be a true American, honest and independent. He felt that adults should have the freedom to choose how they live their lives. As long as you don't hurt anybody you should be able to do whatever you want. Hunter used alcohol and drugs, excessively by most standards but not his own. Everybody has a different tolerance level. Each person must discover what works best for them. Truth is a pathless land. We should all have the freedom to find our own individual truths.

Something was wrong. Besides the events I've produced I've also presented over 4,000 readings of my own work round the world. I know how to read a crowd. The vibrations at The Woody Creek Tavern were not good, they were terrible, gruesome. And it wasn't just because folks were mourning Hunter. I saw right away it was much more than that.

Sarah and I had a delicious meal. We had to sign an I.O.U. for our meal because they don't take credit cards and we didn't have enough cash. We noticed that several others were caught in the same predicament.

Sarah & Ron, Woody Creek Tavern near Hunter's Home, August 20, 2005

As afternoon turned to evening the mood of the growing crowd darkened. There were at least as many members of the world press as there were pilgrims. And nobody, press or pilgrim, was having any luck getting on The List for The Big Party. Nobody could even get on Hunter's property to get a closeup view or photo of the covered statue. I've rarely seen such security. All Friday and Saturday security guards, dressed in black, lined the road from Highway 82 outside Aspen, down across Woody Creek all along Woody Creek Road for miles on each side of Hunter's Owl Farm. Plus security was arm to arm surrounding the property. We drove up to Owl Farm stopping nearby for Sarah to take a photo of me at the Gonzoed mailbox with the Woody Creek Road sign. To our astonishment a huge black SUV drove up to us and stopped. It had GONZO POLICE signs on the sides. It was filled with sneering demon-faced thugs. Sarah had already taken the photo so we walked back to our car. The Gonzo Police drove away. I was astonished. Gonzo Police? Is this possible? Having Gonzo Police patrol a Hunter Thompson party is like me having Poetry Police patrol one of my 48-hour non-stop music and poetry Insomniacathons. It's beyond absurd. It's frightening! The negative energies my increasingly raw nerves were picking up were taking me to a bad bad place.

Ron, Woody Creek, Colorado 2005, photo by Sarah Elizabeth

The spectacle. I have participated in a few glitterati spectacles but I have never been a fan. I can't stand the phoney pomp and circumstance. Although this was an attempt to honor one of the world's greatest writers of all time, a Kentucky rebel with a cause, it had turned into a glitterati rich and famous spectacle much like The Kentucky Derby which Hunter decried in his "The Kentucky Derby is Decadent and Depraved," the piece that birthed Gonzo and forever changed the face of journalism and creative non-fiction. The Blastoff still included family and friends but the rich and famous exclusivity of the event had turned its face ugly, it had grown horns. They were all there to be presented mint juleps at the front tent: John Kerry, George McGovern, Johnny Depp, Bill Murray, Sean Penn, Ralph Steadman, Lyle Lovett, The Nitty Gritty Dirt Band, and so many more. Kind words were said about Hunter, much alcohol was consumed, chandeliers glistened, Japanese drummers drummed then Bob Dylan's "Mr. Tambourine Man," Hunter's favorite song, rang out over loudspeakers, followed by "Spirit In The Sky" as the handsome statue was unveiled, spotlights reflected light off clouds which rested just above the mountains, and Hunter's ashes were blown, with a spectacular light and pyrotechnics show, over his adored Owl Farm.

The difference between The Hunter Blastoff and The Kentucky Derby is that the working class, the poor, the downtrodden have access to The Derby via the infield. The infielders can, if they want, actually fight through the mob to the fence and see the majestic thoroughbreds fly by. The working class, the poor, the downtrodden, the pilgrims who walked, hitchhiked, and drove old broken down vehicles for hundreds and thousands of miles to be close as Hunter's ashes were blasted across his farm well they were not allowed to watch to listen to witness to experience. The event was too exclusive, too precious to even create an infield, to cordon off an area and perhaps even, as part of the $2.5 million production cost, give them boxed wine and potato chips or leftover cake and allow them to be close too so they could also pay homage to their hero, the great Hunter S. Thompson. But they didn't even get that.

As Sarah and I drove up to the main entrance I was in terrible shape. My nerve-shattered extra sensory perception was providing me the most positive glowing warmth while enjoying this adventure with Sarah. But The Blastoff energy was having the opposite effect. The darkness was swallowing me. I was nearly catatonic. Sarah and I have spent our lives as members of and writing for the downtrodden, the beat, the poor, the blue collar working class. In America today the gap between the rich and the poor is greater than ever. I have chosen to be a warrior, a non-violent warrior, against injustice. How could this be happening? What would Hunter think of this spectacle? If Hunter had been assigned to cover The Hunter Blastoff he would have turned and gone back to his hotel room to write The Real Story.

I was overwhelmed by darkness, by the irony that these rich liberals, all of whom condemn Bush for his excessive exclusivity, were being exclusive in the worse possible Marie Antoinette/George Bush way.

We pulled into the main entrance where security checked to see if you were on The List. On the Owl Farm side of Woody Creek Road the see and be seen rich and famous were in the grand tent drinking champagne toasts to their superior status and wealth. On the other side of Woody Creek Road was the mass of pilgrims, and the press, fenced off, forced to keep their distance from the spectacle. We were saddened and sickened by the crude exclusivity of the scene. The energy was totally negative. Pilgrims with hearts full of love and respect for Hunter were treated like second class citizens, literally left out in the cold. As witnesses, Sarah and I, on the verge of nausea, paused at the main entrance, turned, got in our car, with cameras flashing, film crews filming, people yelled "Look, Kentucky, plates!" We fled the scene not wanting to be part of the grotesque snobbery of the glitterati spectacle.

The next morning, Sunday August 21, 2005, we drove back to Owl Farm. Security was still there. We stopped at the main gate and talked with Rich Gilmore, a friendly security guard who promised to visit us in Kentucky. Many Kentuckians and others from other states and countries asked us to say farewell to Hunter for them. We did. Many people in Woody Creek yelled, waved, honked and even followed us because we were the only people there with Kentucky plates. Hunter's life and writing was a continuous series of explosions. He died as he lived, explosion by gun, explosion by cannon. Staring at the fist in the sky I raised a toast to Hunter, "God Bless You & Your Family Hunter, we will meet again." Then Sarah and I drove 24 hours non-stop back to the state we love the most, Kentucky.

published in THE GUIDE, Louisville, Kentucky Fall 2005

Sarah with Security Guard Rich Gilmore at Gonzo Monument Owl Farm, Colorado, August 2005. photo by Ron Whitehead

8
Can Art Matter? Published in Heaven: Blood Filled Vessels

Ron drinking Jesus' blood, Mendocino County, California 2007
photo by Christian Hansen

Can Art Matter?
Published in Heaven: Blood Filled Vessels

The older I get the more I realize I don't know anything, no one does. We're all guessing, feeling our way, grappling for answers. But every day I have encounters with the spirit world. We are all in perpetual motion, in transition, even when we are still, silent, listening. Listening is the greatest art of all. Not-knowing is the fundamental plowed earth of our being, not-knowing. It is our life source. Embrace the wind. Embrace my heart. Born to die, there is no safety, all is demanded. Expose yourself completely. Accept the consequences of your successes, and your failures, as no other dare. Enlightened mind is not special, it is natural. Present yourself as you are, wise fool. Don't hesitate, embrace mystery paradox uncertainty. Have courage. Through fear, and boredom, have faith. Be compassion. Embrace the wind. Embrace your heart. Not-knowing is the fundamental plowed earth of our being. It is our life source. Not-knowing.

Can art matter? Why Published in Heaven?

Today 'Specialization' is sold on every corner, fed in every home, brainwashed into every student, every young person. We are told that the only way to succeed, here at the beginning of the 21st Century is to put all our time, energy, learning, and focus into one area, one field, one specialty (math, science, computer technology, business, government). If we don't we will fail. We are subtly and forcefully, implicitly and explicitly, encouraged to deny the rest of who we are, our total self, selves, our holistic being. The postmodern brave new world resides inside the computer via The Web with only faint peripheral recognition to the person, the individual (and by extension the real global community), the real human being operating the machine. The idea of and belief in specialization as the only path, only possibility, has sped up the fragmentation, the alienation which began to grow rapidly within the individual, radically reshaping culture, over a century ago with the birth of those Machiavellian revolutions in technology, industry, and war. And with the growing fracturing fragmentation and alienation comes the path - anger, fear, anxiety, angst, ennui, nihilism, depression, despair - that, for the person of action, leads to suicide. Unless, through our paradoxical leap of creative faith we engage ourselves in the belief, which can become a life mission that regardless of the consequences, we can, through our engagement, our actions, our loving life work, make the world a better, safer, friendlier place in which to live. Sound naive? What place does the Antinomian voice, the voice that, though trembling, speaks out against The Powers That Be, what place does this Visionary Outsider Voice have in the real violent world in which we are immersed? Are we too desensitized to the violence, to the fact that in the past Century alone we murdered over 160 million people in one war after another, to even think it worthwhile to consider the possibility of a less violent world? Are we too small, too insignificant to make any kind of difference? The power-mongers have control. What difference can one little individual life possibly make possibly matter?

Published in Heaven Titles make a difference. They are blood filled vessels racing to the heart.

Today the X and microserf generations are swollen with young people yearning to express the creative energies buried in their hearts, seeping from every pore of their beings. They ache to change to heal the world. Is it still possible? Is it too late? Is there anyone (a group?) left to show the way to be an example? To be a guide? A mentor? James Joyce, King of Modernism, said the idea of the hero was nothing but a damn lie that the primary motivating forces are passion and compassion. As late as 1984 people were laughing at George Orwell. Today, as we finally move into an Orwellian culture of simulation life on the screen landscape, can we remember passion and compassion or has the postmodern ironic satyric deathinlifegame laugh killed both sperm and egg? Is there anywhere worth going from here? Is it any wonder that today's youth have adopted Jack Kerouac, Allen Ginsberg, William S. Burroughs, Herbert Huncke, Gregory Corso, Neal Cassady, Lawrence Ferlinghetti, Amiri Baraka, Robert Creeley, David Amram,

Diane di Prima, Ed Sanders, Anne Waldman, Bob Dylan, Hunter S. Thompson, The Clash, Sonic Youth and all the other Beat Generation and related poets, writers, artists, musicians as their inspirational, life-affirming antinomian ancestors? These are people who have stood and still stand up against unreasoning power/right/might, looked that power in the eyes and said NO I don't agree with you and this is why. And they have spoken these words, not for money or for fame, but out of life's deepest convictions, out of the belief that we, each one of us, no matter our skin color our economic status our political religious sexual preferences, all of us have the right to live to dream as we choose rather than as some supposed higher moral authority prescribes for us.

I choose to be an antinomian warrior.

Can art matter? Is it merely a gold exchange for the rich? The crucible of Published in Heaven alchemical art blends the terrible beauty of the natural world with questions of global social conscience. Published in Heaven poems stories paintings songs films photographs defy categorization. They are original.

What is involved in the process of artistic creation? And how is that process related to space and time? What makes it possible for a handful of Nabi, of Druidhs, to maneuver in a molecular universe where immersion at will into things and being other than self is readily accomplished, rather than the dreary chore of drudging through the thick cellular world?

The answers are simply complex and like truth, time and water they constantly slip through fingers away away but the past recalled becomes present again and in a sense when we look anywhere including back into the past we are looking with some form of anticipation which is an attribute of future time so where are we really? How do how will poets, writers, painters, sculptors, musicians, filmmakers, photographers creative inhabitors of the creative realms of the 21st Century respond to these questions? Some respond with ironic, comic faith, with passion, with compassion without which the intelligent sensitive creature will inevitably traverse the Valley of The Shadow of Death encountering Angst, Despair, Ennui, and possibly Suicide. The sensitive individual poet writer painter musician filmmaker photographer prophet, the empath whose natural ability is negative capability, ineluctably chooses the life-game quest of self-creation in the possibly infinite probability of possible realities in the self-contained inter-connected Ocean of Consciousness.

So, where are you going? Please answer the question. Can art matter?

There are no answers, only questions.

My argument for The Ocean of Consciousness reaches back to the early experiential understanding of holy while reaching forward beyond the limits of dialectical gnosticism to an alchemy that also transcends divisions inherent in the alienation the fragmentation of Deep Modernism and the superficial chaos of postmodernism. I agree to a point with Turkle's argument that "The goal of healthy personality development is not to become a One, not become a unitary core, it's to have a flexible ability to negotiate the many - cycle through multiple identities." Having multiple identities, being legion, may lead to the apparent conclusion that we are walking on quicksand, that there is no solid ground that all is chaos. Even if you are a cryptanalyst and are able to turn into "plaintext the coded messages of Lacan but also the utterances of French existentialists, deconstructionists, poststructuralists, and all the other sibilant schools that flowed out of postwar France" (McCormick) what leads you to believe that the deadly serious egocentric humor of postmodernism where theory is lauded as more important than text (whatever text might be: book, painting, song, film, life, etc) can possibly be the final word? Deconstructing a text does not designify does not make the text less than what it was before you playfully surgically took it apart and, if you're a good mechanic, put it back together again even if you gave it new features. No matter how much taking apart deconstructing you do there will always remain something, a meaningful essence that cannot be destroyed.

Passion compassion filled art matters.

The poet writer painter musician filmmaker photographer prophet deconstructs realism. She employs the innovative technique of intercalation: the juxtaposition of scenes in time. She is Elus Cohen, Elect Priest of Expressionism, Cubism, Modernism, Dadaism, Surrealism, postmodernism but she is more. She is Master Alchemist, Master Magician. Her long slender hand reaches towards me, grabs my throat, and pulls me into the text, the book, the song, the photo, the painting, the cd/dvd, the film. Manger du Livre indeed! I not only consume the book: the book consumes me. Now I, with her, am Elus Cohen juxtaposing scenes in time and space in her, in me, in the Published in Heaven Blood Filled Vessels Racing to The Heart Titles. Being Blood Filled my original perception, awareness, and senses are fractured, fractaled, and exiting the Blood Filled Heart Titles I find I am rearranged. I now have new perspective, awareness, senses. I look at others. Are their expressions different as they look at me? I must look different. I feel different. I am different. Me. And me now. I,I. Ha. Aha! Now as my hand moves this pen across this page I change. I am transformed. I am never the same. My molecules jump, sway, swoon, dance across the page, giggling, laughing, singing, happy to be new! It's spring again! They shout Yes Yes Yes!!!

Mythopoetic Published in Heaven Titles create newly resonant myths.

Knowledge, from the inception of Modernism and through postmodernism to The Ocean of Consciousness is reorganized, redefined through literature, painting, music, film, photography. The genres are changing, the canons are exploding as is culture. The mythopoetics, the privileged sense of sight, of modern, contemporary, avant-garde poets, writers, musicians, painters, filmmakers, photographers are examples of art forms of a society, a culture, a civilization, a world in which humanity lives, not securely in cities nor innocently in the country, but on the apocalyptic, simultaneous edge of a new realm of being and understanding. The mythopoet, female and male, returns to the role of prophet-seer by creating myths that resonate in the minds of readers, myths that speak with the authority of the ancient myths, myths that are gifts from the creative realms of being, gifts from the shadow.

9
Literary Kicks

Ron & The Porto Shop, Lisbon, Portugal 2007, photo by Xavier Noel

LITERARY KICKS (www.litkicks.com)

by david minton Mar 17, 2002 8:32 PM

Ron Whitehead is a poet with a mission. There aren't enough of those around.

He's been described by Allen Ginsberg as an "energetic Bodhisattvic poetic spirit," by Lawrence Ferlinghetti as "un brave type!," by Douglas Brinkley as "one of the remarkable poets of his generation" (Ron was born in 1950), by Hunter Thompson as "crazy as nine loons."

No doubt about it, Whitehead is a charged and driven charismatic person. His aura of positivity and his Never Give Up attitude --- which the Dalai Lama supernaturally sensed when he imparted the poem of that title Whitehead transcribed and made verse --- are not just perceived but are felt as an irresistible force.

He's a humanist tapped into the Ground Source, a man with a conscience and indomitable spirit, a voice from beyond in the here and now, learning as well as teaching as he travels his path, using poetry as his chosen vehicle. It could have been music, it could have been visual art, but those medium's didn't & don't suit his purpose, which is to rouse as many people as possible -- especially Americans -- out of the big sleep.

Though much of Whitehead's early poetry was designed to tell you about himself as a way of letting you know it's alright to be yourself, he has, since about 1992, decided to become more than an individual beacon of light putting words into books that ultimately languish on library shelves. He's decided to become a visible, helpful, loud-and-clear instigator who is at once actively inspiring and at the same time recruiting already-awake enlightened souls to action against repressive forces of darkness that seek to put the proverbial Orwellian boot on a person's back when that person is down. That person is only down because he or she allows himself or herself to be down and devoid of hope, devoid of The Self. And that person represents the collective person, represents all of us in this world.

Whitehead's call to arms sounds at first revolutionary, but it is essentially basic, heartfelt and intelligent: It's about not conforming to the nationalistic, racist, sexist, evil consumer-producer culture that international governments of the 19th and 20th centuries have sent down to us as our legacy and our collective fate.

The only way to fight those in control, at any given time, is to remain an open, caring and aware individual with a humanist conscience. That's more than just a personal belief --- which becomes poetry ---on Whitehead's part; it is the only effective resistance against what used to be called "the tide of conformity." What Whitehead does in not rabble-rousing; it is the same thing Emerson stood up for, Walt Whitman stood up for, the same thing Gandhi stood up for --- and one telling fact about post-modern world-civilization is clearly seen in the way these people automatically become lightning rods.

Whitehead has come under fire for being anti-American over his 'I Will Not Bow Down' (Hozomeen Press, 1996) and 'Declaration of Independence This Time' (Hozomeen Press, 2001), two savvy works that are as American as apple pie before the apples & grains were mixed with toxic ingredients and baked into a force-fed pastry of imperialist fascism and closed-mindedness by self-serving smug moronic politicians and Puritanical charlatan imbeciles rich enough to advertise themselves as guardians of an inherently detrimental, even deadly, status quo.

Whitehead's agenda is not entirely individualistic, not in the negative sense anyway. He has shaped his persona in such a way as to make of himself an example, James Joyce's "universal in the particular," and the ramifications cause his stance to become political in contemporary society and partly due to the way contemporary governments operate.

Whitehead is decidedly and consciously an Emersonian Kentuckian, a Walt Whitman with a political agenda, philosophizing and yet merely describing the current circumstances, but also offering indispensable pragmatic advice rooted in his own experience of surviving these years since Ronald Reagan and his cronies effectively killed the so-called counter culture of the 1960s.

What Reagan and company didn't count on was that there were true believers among those now derisively called "baby boomers."

Yes, Whitehead was over there in Washington D.C. turning over trash cans on the street in protest of the Vietnam Conflict, dodging tear gas canisters, at the behest of the likes of Jerry Rubin. But Whitehead (and others of his generation) realized that social revolution had already been won by 1973. The Republicans also realized they'd lost that battle for the American conscience by then, and many on both sides of the cultural revolution thought the war was over during the 1970s. The sheep retired, at that time, to New York and Paris discos, with their vials of cocaine, ridiculous clothes, and other leftover surface trappings of "the second revolution." Whitehead himself had found his soul-mate, Nancye, and retired (ca. 1974-78) to his native Beaver Dam, Kentucky, to sell Nissans, the only job available, for an Owensboro dealership and raise a family.

But the post-Nixon governmental backlash was still in the works, and when it hit full-force with Reagan leading the charge, Whitehead was one who decided not to sit around and be discredited for having been a part of the 1960s. He was too much a man to deny that part of himself and retreat to a cloister, a la his much-admired Thomas Merton, and, anyway, Whitehead had snake-handling holy-rollers in his ancestry. Total defeat is inadmissible to him; self-emasculation is not in his nature.

His option, he felt, was academia, and he enrolled at the University of Louisville around 1980, finding a mentor in Dr. Joe Slavin. Slavin encouraged him not only to consider teaching as a profession, but also to write, something Whitehead had had in the back of his own mind since childhood but had, like many writers, only trifled with and not considered seriously as a profession. He was instantaneously sparked by his studies and Slavin's suggestion, and ended up taking over editorship of Thinker Review, the university's student publication. Using his car-salesman skills, he talked U of L out of a previously unheard-of $15,000 budget, and he modeled the resulting publication on The Chicago Review and Triquarterly. The book was a resounding success, and his tenure as editor was extended. For the second Thinker Review, he contacted a multitude of nationals and internationals, and scored a huge coup: he got Seamus Heaney to contribute a pre-Nobel Prize poem, along with contributions from Diane di Prima, Lucien Stryk and Eithne Strong. He also made a contact with Allen Ginsberg, and ended up bringing Ginsberg to Louisville for a reading.

Ginsberg proved ultimately to be a lifelong ally and friend. And it was not a matter of Whitehead riding on the famous author's coat tails.

Ginsberg had, by 1979, been reduced to getting himself featured in People magazine sitting on railroad tracks blocking trains from delivering nuclear wastes here and there.

Once the Whitehead-Ginsberg contact was made, it morphed into a friendly symbiotic relationship. Ginsberg lent his name and his then-shrinking credibility to Whitehead's efforts at organizing readings and his inroads into publishing. Ginsberg also turned Whitehead on to his insider list of contacts. Whitehead jumped waist-deep into the reviving of Ginsberg's lagging career as a poet, though at the time it seemed a daunting task for a complete unknown like himself, but he did manage to inspire Ginsberg to start howling at pulpits and lecterns again instead of spending so much of his time on photography and on getting himself arrested for belated ineffectual protests and playing the victim.

Whitehead's causes and plans of action were unformulated at the time, but he was soon finding his feet, after much soul-searching and a lot of knocking on doors he had been pointed to by Ginsberg.

Whitehead's personal ideology, rooted in much-maligned teachings of Ram Dass, in literary treatises found in novels such as Knut Hamsun's Hunger, in Edvard Munch's profoundly expressionist paintings and prints, in music from Bill Monroe to the Grateful Dead and Sonic Youth, soon became fully integrated with a crystal-clear understanding of what Abbie Hoffman had tried to accomplish; with an intimation of what past sages (from prophets to our own Thomas Jefferson) had been up against; with what documents such as the United Nations' Declaration of Human Rights stand for in real time as applicable declarations and not just as a hopeful but to-be-disregarded ideals.

Everything Whitehead had ever learned or had intuitively known fell into place by the mid-1990s. He was inevitably moved to take action --- not only to write books, but also to tie himself to a socially submerged upheaval that he was surprised to find was happening all over the United States and Europe. He has emerged, subsequently, as a leader in that underground, though it is not his intention to be a leader. His intention is only to instigate awakening among those who wish to awaken, to kick in the ass or tweak the cheeks of those who would have others sleepwalk through lifetimes:

The falcon cannot hear the falconer;
Things fall apart; the centre will not hold;
The power-mongers are loosed upon the world;
The ceremony of innocence is drowned;
The best lack all conviction, while the worst
are full of passionate intensity.   -- from 'The Reformation'

These words are partly appropriated from William Butler Yeats, doctored of course, and Whitehead "dedicates" his co-opted rendering to "The Fathers Who Art Round(Heads)" -- by name: Rush Limbaugh, George Bush, Pat Robertson, Kenneth Starr.

That such a writing would be considered dangerous or threatening, and could potentially draw down the wrath of American elected officials, speaks for itself and shows us how drastically and dramatically

America, in particular and as an entity, has been circumvented and perverted. Whitehead is keenly aware that basic American freedoms are disappearing rapidly as we enter the 21st century.

"She is cast from the garden into what she thinks are dreams, nightmares. She attempted to accelerate the qualitative growth of the animal race. She slept with one who was superior to the rest. Centuries of teaching had gotten nowhere, but with Canto's admixture she could change that. Did she deceive herself? Had she been deceived? Nothing is clear..." -- from 'White Horses'

One of Whitehead's quests involves an articulation of 'The Ocean of Consciousness', in order to tap mankind into "the qualitative growth" that will make us truly civilized.

'Blood Filled Vessels Racing To The Heart' (Hozomeen Press, 1997) was an attempt to explain the Ocean of Consciousness in apolitical terms. Unfortunately, it fails as a manifesto because it speaks academically instead of pragmatically. There is much finger-pointing toward as-yet unrealized historical ideas of merit, and the implication that these ideas can be realized partially redeems the text.

'The Beaver Dam Rocking Chair Marathon' (unfinished as of this February 2002 writing, except for volume one, issued by Tilt-A-Whirl Press, 1998) goes further toward articulating this Ocean of Consciousness, to which we all belong but are taught by social institutions and governments to deny in order to perpetuate feelings of hopelessness and alienation that keep a galvanized and earth-shaking irrevocable spiritual and political revolution from occurring.

Whitehead finds himself, in 2002, as a link between the Beats, Scandinavian expressionists of the late 19th and early 20th centuries, European poets in the tradition of Yeats to Heaney, modernist writers such as James Joyce and Ezra Pound, and so-called Generation Xers and now Generation Post-Xers, whom he has been professor to during the 1980s and 1990s and is still teaching in the first decade of century

21. Along the way, he's linked arms with other inter-generational luminaries (and I use the term "luminaries" not in the sense of celebrity, but instead in its literal sense) such as Casey Cyr and Bob Holman.

"Many times I've thought I needed to move to New York or San Francisco to make myself heard," Whitehead said to me once, "but Ferlinghetti told me there was no need for that, that I was already making myself heard based right here in Louisville [Kentucky]. And I have a love-hate relationship with Kentucky, but it was no different when I lived in Reykjavik [Iceland] for two years. I still had to travel to Netherlands and read in Amsterdam, still had to travel to Wisconsin and New York and New Orleans to read. So no matter where I live, I'd still have to travel, just like the Rolling Stones have to travel, which I don't mind at all. I'm a restless spirit anyway."

The books are out there. They're on the shelves at City Lights, on the shelves in Chicago, on the shelves in Portugal and India. So are the books of others he's published since founding the Kentucky-based Literary Renaissance in 1992.

Literary Renaissance has imported writers, artists and musicians to Kentucky, and has exported Midwestern Americans to points all over the globe. The idea is to pinpoint individuals and groups with something to transmit and help them make themselves heard --- on a stage, in bars and cafes, in auditoriums at universities, on the radio, through CD releases as well as books. He finds the avenues, and he speaks and he brings others along with him to speak and play music and otherwise communicate worthy ideas or statements.

A subsidiary of Literary Renaissance is Published in Heaven, an outfit that has published and continues to publish a series of chapbooks as well as poems and visuals on posters and including material by everyone from Grateful Dead lyricist Robert Hunter to Yoko Ono to former American President Jimmy Carter.

Whitehead has also been a tireless organizer of reading and music events since the 1980s. His "Insomniacathons," which sometimes go for three or four days nonstop, are now legendary.

These events and CDs take the word off the page and make them real, while leaving the pages and CDs for history, in case history's interested.

Lots of writers don't know how to get out of their own vacuums. They're not fit for society or society rejects them for one reason or another. Society puts them in this quandary and the result is a standoff: They want to deal with everything second-hand, through their writings. They can't or don't know how to deal with the reality of what's happening. Again, this is something the so-called Status Quo requires of all citizens, all who would fit into the "normal scheme of things."

Whitehead doesn't fit into that normal scheme of things, and he's not willing to retreat and forget it, because he knows that "normalcy," as it is generally conceived of, is a political and social ploy that keeps individuals from being shining examples of humanity in the Christian, Buddhist, Taoist, Hindu or even Agnostic reality.

He writes his blasts against dangerous political idiocy, he writes his contagious love poems, he co-opts what makes sense to him and passes it on in the same way those before him have, like shamans, passed on what is valuable -- then he bothers to hit the road and read it to people, face to face, to meet his audience and other poets on similar quests, instead of just tapping it into a computer file and letting a newspaper or book publisher send out sanitized reviews which either fall upon deaf ears or circumvent the real message. He interacts with people, is a citizen diplomat, finds some who are in common cause with him, ends up arguing wrestling with others who aren't.

But he's unstoppable now that he knows what his mission is:

What world have we born ourselves into?
Do we have a wrestling, not against blood and

flesh but against governments, against authorities,
against world rulers, rulers of darkness, against wicked spirit forces in
heavenly places?

What world have we born ourselves into?
Should we put on the suit of armor from God?

Stand firm with out loins girded with truth?
Is this where the intelligence that is wisdom comes in? Seven heads
mean seven mountains?

What world have we born ourselves into?

-- from 'What World Have We Born Ourselves Into: The Apocalypse Rag'

The World Ambassador of Poetry[1]

By Annalisa Papaleo

from her book "Ron Whitehead : a beat voice in the Kentucky of XXI century"

> *Forget safety*
> *Live where you fear to live*
> *Destroy your reputation*
> *Be notorious*
> *I have tried prudent planning*
> *Long enough. From now*
> *On, I'll be mad.*[2]

Whitehead is the author of numerous books, poems and anthologies, which are correlated to The Beat tradition but still rooted with originality and individuality.

Because his poetry doesn't have a recurrent or specific theme, the characteristics are difficult to define or categorize.

His spirit is open and sensitive to every artistic and creative matter. He is continually inspired by daily experience. The result is the image of a poet par excellence, who always hears the inspiring muse of the moment, giving birth to immediate poetry that has been lived.

Being completely free from every scheme or poetic rule, he can deliberately choose to be formal or informal, serious or engaged and comical or ironic simultaneously.

Without abandoning linguistic forms which may seem too elaborated and sophisticated, his poems talk about love, Zen, meditation, politics, violence, sex, America and the green Kentucky.

---

[1] Michael Odin Pollock, http://www.tappingmyownphone.com/Testimonials.html, the 05.05.04.

[2] Whithead Ron, *Beaver Dam Rocking Chair Marathon,* books I and II, Wasteland Press, Louisville, KY, USA, 2002.

Every poem is created under fresh and different clothing and always deeply original.

I can establish some general lines with which to create an ideological and thematic background for his work and with which to reflect on Ron's individuality and personality:

> *fearless compassionate honesty, non-violent fighting against injustice, life as it is, no disneyfication, terrible beauty.*[3]

Ron always lived with poetry; life itself, for him, is art. It's not stupefying that he defines daily living as an artistic work.

So, if poetry is art, what is the role of the poet? What instruments are at his creative disposal?

Whitehead, the poet-prophet, reveals to us how and where we, as human beings and society, are wandering, moving continuously from past to present while still in future's direction. His poetry tells what could happen, revealing it with a fine voice and a delicate breath.

Ron, above all, sees what we hear and therefore renders him, The Poet, the bearer of sight.

For this reason, most of Whitehead's poems follow the same mystical and prophetical direction, having themes and styles different form each other. What strikes us is the way he includes the divine in the ordinary, turning magical a simple fragment of daily life giving it a universal value.

Whitehead is a prophet because he's a person who understands, with the senses and experience, what is hidden behind an apparent signification, which is its enigma and which is the deep and occult meaning it hides. He is a prophet because he believes and knows that the truth can be understood across the spirit and instinct. That truth is independent from our mind and operates autonomously. Again, he's a prophet because everything is ultimately pure and he transforms complexities of life into pure acts, poetry, with strong symbolic value.

---

[3] http://www.tappingmyownphone.com/ITKYandBeyond.pdf, the 10.05.04

All this is reflected in his poetry with a direct and simple style that is understandable and melodious. Because Ron is aware that every person has the need for poetry, the desire to discover the secret of life and its mysteries, he is the spokesperson of this unknown world, awakening the poet inside all of us.

His work is always at least exciting if not magical. It is simultaneously hard-bitten, stark and urban while containing a gentle, pastoral lyricism all of which is always compelling. His work is a dharma gate that must be entered, a magnificent Zen koan where the question and answer lie hidden in the experience[4].

The most symbolic of all his collection of poems is *Never Give Up*, written after having met His Holiness The Dalai Lama in 1994.

His spirituality, sensitivity and meditative traits have always been consistent but after having met The Dalai Lama his personal and artistic existence underwent a strong intensification. It was not a revelation but an awareness of his already started mission and a confirmation and justification of his individuality regarding humanity and the spreading of his message of love and peace.

Ron's poem was born from a message of simple existence and perseverance, given to him by His Holiness. It will become a motto and an internal rule for everyone with whom he came in contact.

"Develop the heart

Too much energy in your country

Is spent developing the mind

Instead of the heart

Develop the heart."[5]

---

[4] http://www.tappingmyownphone.com/Testimonials.html, the 10.05.04
[5] http://www.tappingmyownphone.com/NGU.html, the 15.05.04.

Besides a mystical note, a thin line of romance marks Whitehead's poetry. It is a love poem of pure and total love, addressed to the entire universe and embracing everything it envelopes.

He's a poet tenderly enraged, who, with delicateness and decision, knows where to point his finger and how to create a song of revolt, protest and engagement. Fundamentally, Whitehead is the new singer of America, who addresses American politics without giving false ideologies or taking sides; he's the singer of his green land, of his local colours and of his tradition.

His simple and chasing racing style, without a breath, shows us: vices, virtues, pains, regrets, fame, failures, values and corruption of his America.

> *Ron explodes in a tirade aimed at pulling down all the garbage that society holds dear: rampant commercialism couldn't care lessism.*
>
> *If the President thinks he's got trouble with Ms Lewinsky then he'd better watch out for Ron as he gives us the real character of the real America.*[6]

It would not be a mistake to affirm that Whitehead, with his passive way to react, to rebel and to denounce all established roles imposed by society is lacerating, little by little like a small sharp knife, the bones of American society.

The poems *I Will Not Bow Down* and *The Declaration of Independence This Time* represent the height of this revolt, because "the dissent is not un-American", as centuries of barbarism and oppression made us believe; he will never be submissive but will always carry on his non-violent protest in the name of love for his country and all who live in it:

---

[6] Ring Kevin http://www.tappingmyownphone.com/Testimonials.html, the 15.05.04. He is the editor, from years, of a magazine published in England, *Beat Scene*, which brings on the reins of a tradition with articles, poems, interviews and reviews. It's thank to Mr Ring and to his suggest that I knew Ron Whitehead, who will soon appear, as in the past, in his magazine.

I will not Bow Down America
to your invasion of privacy
to your moral absolutes

America
I pledge allegiance
to the woman I love
and to our children
I pledge allegiance
to my friends and allies
my guides and angels
both seen and unseen.[7]

His poems reach the heart of America's lost souls, who suffer the lack of something in the beginning of century, while continuing the rebellion of Beat writers, proposing new poetic and literary manifestos towards a new era that is slowly defeating the walls of hypocrisy. His poems break down barriers in order for us to find ourselves as humans.

---

[7] http://www.tappingmyownphone.com/Bowdown.pdf, the 10.05.04

# The World Ambassador of Poetry[8]

By Annalisa Papaleo

Italian: "Ron Whitehead : una voce beat nel Kentucky del XXI secolo"

Forget safety
Live where you fear to live
Destroy your reputation
Be notorious
I have tried prudent planning
Long enough. From now
On, I'll be mad[9]

Whitehead è l'autore di numerose raccolte di poesie, di antologie che si ricollegano alla più vera tradizione *beat* ma imperniate di originalità e di individualità.

La sua poetica non ha una tematica ricorrente e specifica alla quale egli fa riferimento; di conseguenza, non possiamo dare una definizione netta sul carattere della sua poesia.

Il suo è uno spirito aperto e sensibile a qualsiasi forma artistica e creativa ed è continuamente ispirato dall'esperienza quotidiana; ne deriva l'immagine del poeta per eccellenza, di colui che, come egli stesso ha affermato, ascolta sempre la sua musa ispiratrice sul momento, dando vita ad una poesia immediata e vissuta.

Essendo completamente libero da ogni schema o da regole poetiche, egli può liberamente scegliere di essere formale o informale, serio e impegnato o comico e ironico al tempo stesso.

---

[8] Michael Odin Pollock, http://www.tappingmyownphone.com/Testimonials.html, il 05.05.04.
[9] Whitehead Ron, *Beaver Dam Rocking Chair Marathon,* books I and II, Wasteland Press, Louisville, KY, USA, 2002.

Le sue sono poesie che parlano dell'amore, dello zen, della mediazione, della politica e della violenza, del sesso, dell'America e della sua verde terra, il Kentucky, ogni volta sotto fresche vesti differenti, profondamente originali, senza abbandonarsi a forme linguistiche troppo ideologicamente e stilisticamente elaborate.

Tuttavia, dopo una loro attenta lettura, è possibile stabilire delle linee molto generali che fanno da sfondo ideologico e tematico alle sue opere e che riflettono l'individualità e la personalità del poeta:

> *fearless compassionate honesty, non-violent fighting against injustice, life as it is, no disneyfication, terrible beauty*[10]

Ron ha sempre vissuto di poesia; la vita stessa per lui è arte. Non stupisce quindi che egli definisca tutto ciò che vive quotidianamente come un'opera artistica.

Se la poesia è, quindi, un arte, quale deve essere il ruolo del poeta? Quali sono gli strumenti a sua disposizione?

Secondo Whitehead, il poeta-profeta ci rivela come e dove noi individui, e le società, andiamo errando, in continuo spostamento dal passato al presente e diretti verso un futuro; è colui che può dirci cosa potrebbe succedere, rivelandocelo con una sottile voce e un delicato sospiro.

È soprattutto colui che vede quello che noi sentiamo: essere un poeta è vedere.

Per questo la maggior parte delle poesie di Whitehead seguono la stessa linea mistica e profetica, pur avendo tematiche e stili differenti: quello che colpisce è il suo modo di includere il divino nell'ordinario, di rendere magico un semplice frammento di vita quotidiana e di attribuirgli un valore universale.

Whitehead è un profeta, essendo una persona che comprende, sensorialmente e con l'esperienza, cosa è nascosto dietro un apparente

---

[10] http://www.tappingmyownphone.com/ITKYandBeyond.pdf, il 10.05.04

significato, quale è il suo enigma e quale è il significato profondo e occulto che lo cela; è un profeta perché crede e sa che la verità può essere conosciuta attraverso lo spirito, l'istinto e che è indipendente dalla nostra mente ma opera a livello autonomo. È ancora un profeta perché tutto è puro e il profeta sa trasformare le complessità della vita in atti puri e con forte valenza simbolica.

Tutto questo viene riflesso nella sua poesia con uno stile semplice e diretto, comprensibile e melodioso perché Ron è convinto che ogni uomo ha vivo e forte dentro di sé il bisogno di poesia, il desiderio di scoprire, quando possibile, i segreti della vita e i suoi misteri, e, per ultimo, il compito del poeta è quello di farsi portavoce di questo mondo ignoto, di svegliare il poeta che è in noi.

> *His work is always at least exciting if not magical. It is simultaneously hard-bitten, stark and urban while containing a gentle, pastoral lyricism all of which is always compelling. His work is a dharma gate that must be entered, a magnificent Zen koan where the question and answer lie hidden in the experience*[11].

Una poesia-simbolo di tutte le sue raccolte è *Never Give Up*, scritta dopo l'incontro con sua santità il Dalai Lama, avvenuta nel 1994.

Come ho appena affermato, la sua spiritualità e i suoi tratti lievemente sensistici e meditativi, sono sempre stati delle costanti nella sua attività ma dopo aver incontrato il Dalai Lama, l'esperienza personale e artistica di Whitehead ha subito una forte intensificazione: non è stata una rivelazione ma solo una presa di coscienza della missione già iniziata e una conferma di quanto fosse giusto il suo operare individualmente per la collettività e il diffondere il suo messaggio di amore e di pace.

---

[11] http://www.tappingmyownphone.com/Testimonials.html, il 10.05.04

La poesia infatti è nata proprio da un messaggio di operare e non arrendersi mai, datogli da sua santità, e che ormai è diventato un motto ed una regola interiore per tutti coloro che ne sono venuti a contatto.

Develop the heart
Too much energy in your country
Is spent developing the mind
Instead of the heart
Develop the heart.[12]

Oltre al misticismo la poetica di Whitehead è marcata da una sottile vena romantica; la sua è una poesia principalmente d'amore, un amore puro e totale, indirizzata all'intero universo e che abbraccia tutto ciò che esso ingloba.

È un poeta teneramente arrabbiato, che con delicatezza e decisione sa dove puntare il dito e fare della sua poesia un canto di rivolta, di protesta, di impegno.

Fondamentalmente Whitehead è il nuovo cantore dell'America, che lascia assaporare il gusto della politica americana senza dare false ideologie o senza assumere prese di posizione; è il cantore della sua verde terra, dei suoi colori locali e delle sue tradizioni.

Il suo è uno stile semplice ma incalzante, senza respiro, che ci mostra, vizi e virtù, dolori e dispiaceri, fama e fallimenti, valori e corruzioni della sua America.

Ron explodes in a tirade aimed at pulling down all the garbage that society holds dear: rampant commercialism, couldn't care lessism.

If the President thinks he's got trouble with Ms Lewinsky then he'd better watch out for Ron as he gives us the real caracter of the real America.[13]

---

[12] http://www.tappingmyownphone.com/NGU.html, il 15.05.04.
[13] Ring Kevin http://www.tappingmyownphone.com/Testimonials.html, il 15.05.04. Egli è l'editore da anni di una rivista che viene pubblicata in Inghilterra, *Beat Scene*, che porta avanti le redini di una tradizione con articoli, poesie,interviste e recensioni. È stato proprio grazie a

Potremmo affermare che con il suo modo di ribellarsi pacificamente, di reagire e non accettare passivamente i ruoli prestabiliti della società che limiterebbero e annullerebbero la propria persona, Whitehead sta lacerando poco alla volta, come una lama sottile, affilata e impercettibile, le ossa della società americana.

Le poesie *I Will Not Bow Down* e *The Declaration of Indipendence This Time* rappresentano il culmine di questa rivolta, poiché il dissenso non è anti-americano, come secoli di barbarie e oppressione hanno portato a far credere; egli non si piegherà mai ai suoi piedi ma porterà avanti la sua lotta non violenta per amore di questa terra stessa e di tutta la gente che l'abita:

> *I will not Bow Down America*
> *to your invasion of privacy*
> *to your moral absolutes*
>
> *America*
> *I pledge allegiance*
> *to the woman I love*
> *and to our children*
> *I pledge allegiance*
> *to my friends and allies*
> *my guides and angels*
> *both seen and unseen*[14]

Le sue poesie giungono fino al cuore dell'America, e negli animi di chi vive una perdita, di chi soffre per la mancanza di qualcosa in questo inizio del nuovo millennio, e, portando avanti il carattere di ribellione degli scrittori della *beat generation*, propone dei nuovi manifesti poetici e letterari di una nuova epoca che sta abbattendo lentamente i muri dell'ipocrisia, per vedere e trovare finalmente, oltre le barriere, un carattere più umano e solidale in ognuno di noi.

Mister Ring e ad un suo consiglio, che sono entrata in contatto con Ron Whitehead,
[14] http://www.tappingmyownphone.com/Bowdown.pdf, il 10.05.04

Watching With a Thousand Eyes

by Casey Cyr

When Ron Whitehead formed his poetic musical ensemble The Viking Hillbilly Apocalypse Revue, in 2001, I thought he might be pushing it. Apocalypse? What was he talking about? In 2005, as America backslides like a mercury retrograde fireball toward the 15th century, I can only nod in acceptance. Ron Whitehead was sent here for a reason, which turns out to be many interconnected reasons, ever unfolding. Ron Whitehead is Visionary, Peacemaker, Champion of Truth.

Can we separate the works from the man? Insomniacathon is but one outward manifestation of his creative force, ever urging onward. Without this outward motion, all would implode from its fiery creation storm. Ink and paper are not enough. They cannot contain this radiant ethereal language. If Ron Whitehead ever stops moving, don't be surprised if he goes up in a burst of flames. Or tell the light to stand still!

Ron Whitehead is Uniter like Shiva who reveals his purposes as the great Destroyer of illusion. "His dance of bliss represents creation as well as destruction, and is for the welfare of the world. While giving darshan (the grace-bestowing view of Divinity) to his devotees, within the Hall of Consciousness, which is the heart of man, he crushes the demon of ignorance (forgetting), called Aspasmara Pursha."

His darshan: poem. His devotees: poets. His faces, tiger: mind, fire: destruction, and ultimately creation. From his ashes: the formation of a new universe. Yes, Ron Whitehead can destroy centuries of untruths in one fell swoop with his pen, and rebuild with his Blood Filled Vessels Racing to the Heart from his poetic darshan to his poet devotees within the great hall of consciousness.

Since the formation of the Apocalypse Revue, earthquakes, fires, floods, hurricanes, tsunami and war have escalated in number and scope. America's current political atmosphere suggests the dismantling of a just democracy by diminishing human rights, civil liberties, freedom of expression and privacy. OK! Apocalypse it is. Who knew the pendulum would swing so violently wrong? Apparently Ron Whitehead.

When I met Ron in 1995, at the The Writings of Jack Kerouac Conference at New York University when Rich Martin and I were peddling our books with Hozomeen Press, I knew Ron's I Will Not Bow Down was an astonishing visionary masterwork. At least several decades ahead of its time, it spoke of the individual in the deepest sense. Ron's incredible mind electrically charged, synapses firing at a million miles an hour, yet somehow suspended in time, echoing a timeless eternity transposed on our technological wonderland that would lead to our superconnected yet conversely disconnected state of humanity. What Guts, not bravado, Guts! What nerve! To expose us so! What vision! What truth!

So, when Ron's next manuscript was sent to Hozomeen Press, you would think that I would have known better. But, alas, The Declaration of Independence This Time threw Martin and me for a loop. "Its great!!!" "But what about the title?" "He's using the actual name of The Declaration in there." Humm... We didn't know what to make of it but ultimately said: "He's the artist and we've gotta go with the artist's vision." End of story. Trust with the soul. Sometimes you gotta trust before you understand.

Last night I creaked up the long staircase to my attic with flashlight. I found my old box of treasures from that time. Among those treasures was a Tribe Magazine featuring the 1996 Insomniacathon in New Orleans, that I had the honor of participating in. The last line from Douglas Brinkley's "Dehydrated Dawns At Cafe Du Monde" confirms a perspective we can know somewhere between the heart and solar plexus: "ART is all we can trust."

We can only ponder the tragic remains of the Constitution after yet another Supreme Court Justice from Modern Rome circa 1425 joins the bench. Who knew that things would get this desperate? That the Declaration of Independence might as well be scrap-heap kindling since the radical right took over? Apparently Ron Whitehead, that's who! In stark, deep contrast to our leaders responsible for such a backwards downturn, Ron's about 200 years ahead of HIS time. It will take that long for the majority to become enlightened and to value the individual enough to make it a mandate. And yes, rewrite the Declaration of Independence, and the Constitution all over again. Thanks Ron, for leading the way.

The Apocalypse has been previewed. The Declaration of Independence has finally been written in it's entirety. As for The Third Testament: Three Gospels of Peace, which includes 3 of Ron's Masterpieces, I don't know about you but I'm getting my helmet on. This is gonna be a doozie. These 3 volumes, read in succession, are so potent they are 3,000 years ahead of schedule. When the world would take that long to allow any additions to our sacred documents, their exclusions exposed, their illusions destroyed, Ron already knows. Our hallowed texts do need revisiting, reinterpretation, and ultimately an increase in the scope of love and acceptance not nearly thought of by mankind.

Only one who prefers inclusion would ever arrive at this conclusion. Yes, Ron is just as keen on Jesus as he is on Shiva. I don't think there are any aspects of God that Ron would deny. Or cultures he would have burn in hell because of their exclusion. This is the enlightened path. In more enlightened cultures, God is already here! Bhagavan Sri Sathya Sai Baba says: "There is only one religion, the religion of Love, Honor all religions. Each is a pathway to God." His devotees are ready for the Incarnation of God, Living, and Sathya Sai Baba walks among them. Maybe Jesus hasn't come again because too many of his devotees are still asleep? Shiva strikes down the ignorance of forgetting. They don't use the word evil. Forgetting your divinity creates distance from God. A more enlightened concept.

If the Third Testament is the Gospel, Insomniacathon is the Rapture! How would Jesus deny one woman over another in need of food or water? Ron Whitehead, Destroyer of Illusion, Champion of Truth, doesn't really have any choice! How could there be any ROOM for exclusion, when the only answer is INCLUSION? When it comes to the way Insomniacathon has been run, with it's enormity, it's vastness, it's inclusiveness, Ron Whitehead has always remained true to himself, and to his enlightened purpose and vision. Enlightenment doesn't function in reverse. And, one cannot discuss the works without discussing the man! Try to take the heart out of the lion!

For Ron, who walks incarnate while dwelling in enlightenment, the greatest sacrifice is a time slot that is not available for a voice. The only anguish I have ever heard from Ron was anguish for those artists he could not squeeze in. For books he could not publish due to financial reasons, for others, not himself! Ron's wish, as I have observed it in years past, was that there were more hours in a day, and more enlightened venue managers who understood that Insomniacathon would require a great deal of stage time.

I learned a couple of other things about Insomniacathon. One thing's for sure, they don't call Ramblin' Jack Elliot ramblin for nothin! I was the last reader on the last day of Insomniacathon at the Contemporary Arts Center in New Orleans 1996. I was anxious as my time approached, as I knew the venue would be closing soon. But alas, Jack left the stage just in time for me to read from View From the Launch Pad, with David Amram accompanying me on 2 flutes!! at once! Jack was really a ramblin angel just testing me, to see just how important I thought I was. My poem was read in its entirety. The last page reads:

City Lights, New Directions, Hozomeen,
(that's Hose-oh-meeen sez Ginsberg)
White Fields Press

O heaven
she keeps whispering

she keeps ranting
her song out

know the song
of the world

know the song
from worlds in heaven

O the light of heaven
and O the darkness of heaven
she sends her angels down
one dark and one light
by truth which in it
must account for illusion

to reckon
the last holy war
that takes us on
individually

how do i learn to love

As I read the last word, "love," they shut off my microphone and the lights. The Arts Center had no idea my piece was ending then, they just had to close up shop. Apparently, love IS the last word.

Ron embraced me afterwards and said he was so happy that I got to read at the Arts Center. He would have gladly let me read at Howlin' Wolf later that night, if I lost my time slot there. That's how it's always been with Ron. He's happier to give than anything else. Ron, Keeper of the Flame, Destroyer of Illusion, Akin and Partner to David Amram, Champion of Inclusion Not Before Seen, We See YOU.

Acknowledgment must come before Enlightenment. Buddha, Jesus, Sathya Sai Baba can appear before us but we will not see or hear if our hearts are not ready. How many Poet Hearts has Ron made ready? So that they can contribute to the vast chain of awakening humanity like thousands of silver threads from the light of heaven?

When I co-founded the New York Underground Music and Poetry Festival in 2000 with Ron, David Amram, Nora Edison and Mike McHugh, he brought this message: Never Give Up. Develop the Heart. Be Compassionate. Work for Peace in the World and In Your Heart. No Matter What is Going On Around You, Never Give Up. Passed from His Holiness The Dalai Lama to Ron Whitehead, and to us. The Dalai Lama knew Ron would be opening many hearts, freeing many voices, awakening much compassion. He also knew we would be facing many hardships. Intuitive knowing. Ahead of time, and right on time. I can only be thankful that I was ready to hear it.

The Divine Energy of His Holiness The Dalai Lama trusted in Ron Whitehead, "one of the great poets of his generation" (Douglas Brinkley); "Crazy as Nine Loons" (Hunter Thompson); "World Ambassador of Poetry" (Michael Pollock); "sowing the dragon's teeth of new heroics" (Lawrence Ferlinghetti).

Accolades abound for Ron's tremendous accomplishments, but the GREATEST one, and what sets him distinctly apart is this: Ron adamantly insists on ascending to the top of the mountain bringing thousands, millions if he can, with him. He Lifts Up His Generation. He's not afraid to share the Light of Endless Abundance, that he realizes is Endless!!! There's nothing to worry about. You can come in. You can speak. You are welcome. Ron makes his space, in this time, a home for us. If he takes you by the hand, you'd be better off to follow. It's one hell of a ride!

Don't be surprised at some faraway time, to see Ron Whitehead (and probably Corso too) lurking somewhere near Peter at the Gates of Heaven, urging "just a few more, just a few more," Let Them In! I'll tell you what, If that don't work, I volunteer to assist Ron in setting up The Holy Back Door of Forgiveness. I think that's a secret meaning of Ron's

AHA! He'll get you Secret Sacred Directions, lightening speed. The Underground has its purposes.

In my box of treasures from my attic I found a manuscript page with Ron's notations. Neatly in the same box, right next to my lost NYU papers I was scouring the house for, to find the correct conference title. I didn't know where they were. There are a hundred boxes. Ten years later, right on time, it was all there. Just like Sathya Sai Baba, who walked right on my bus going up 8th Avenue, sat down next to me and said everything without saying a word. But that's another story...

"last poem of book,
For as long as space endures
prayer for the living

Last stanza:

For as long as space endures
And for as long as living beings remain,
Until then may I too abide, despite my failures,
To dispel the misery of the world.

Ron Whitehead, 10-06-95 revised 10-07-95"

"The Lord will be watching with a thousand eyes the least activity of man to discover any slight trace of selfless love sweetening it."
Bhagavan Sri Sathya Sai Baba.

Alfama   old Lisbon   Portugal   February 2007
a love poem

for Sarah

    visited Iris and Xavier
    flew from Louisville to Detroit to London to Lisbon
    my longtime dear friend Lucia and Maria and Pedro
    and their dog
            picked us up
    drove us   in their natural gas powered Peugeot
    ancient friendly wisdomeyed
       dog by my side in my lap front seat
       to Alfama   to old Lisbon
       Escolas Gerais #24-2
       Iris and Xavier's apartment
       narrow streets   centuries old
       cobblestones handmade
       tram rails electric   electrico 28
       trams unlike any other orange and lemon colored trams
       painted paintings trams decades
           centuries old in mint condition
       trams dance slowly up and down narrow old Lisbon
          cobbled streets   clothes hanging stories high
                              stories high
       three four five stories   every street
          filled with stories myths alive
       fairy tale streets stories the clothes tell
                  in gentle rain in turquoise
       sunshine and fog on Rio Tejo foghorns ships
           boats headed to and fro
       river ocean   Tejo Atlantic   mists in the morning
           church bells and trams
       at 5am   pigeons loving rooftops singing dawn

      Sarah and I sleep on the top floor
         on the futoned floor   under the stars
    the night sky our window   door to the moon
at 2am   after Fado Fado beautiful Fado
           we wander meander down and up
narrow stairs streets alleys   Sarah says   listen
     listen   and we all
Iris and Xavier and Sarah and I all stop
     and listen we listen   we listen
and all we hear is the sound the soft and gentle
         sound of   silence   silence
at 2am   Alfama   old Lisbon   no sounds no dogs
   barking   no horns blowing
no church bells singing no cars grinding no
         boats no   planes no   talking
only   silence silence silence   stillness   at 2am
    in old Lisbon   what beauty
no other city in the world can say   silence   at 2am
   no   sound   only
         silence   stillness   silence
I take Sarah's hand   we kiss   gentle   on lips
   we melt   at 2am   old Lisbon
     in the mist in the silent rain   we kiss
Xavier plays gypsy violin while preparing
           gourmet French and Portuguese
dishes   rare spices herbs   delicious   the food
    melts in   our mouths
the music melts our hearts   Rimbaud
   Apollinaire   Jacques Brel   French songs poems
of love of peace of friendship   Xavier is
    the best   tour guide in
Portugal   watch out for the trams   step into
   a doorway   or die
spring is here   orange and lemon trees pregnant with
        ripe fruit
at Portugal's largest bizarre   street market

                block after   block after   block
                Xavier says look   and there   lo and behold
                           there we see   a tree   filled
                with big bright green glowing green parrots
                                         never before the people say
                never before has such a sight been seen
                           global warming   they say   has
                has   has   global warming has thrown off
                           their migratory patterns the birds
                the green birds look over the bizarre
                      and in unison yell   further   further
                further   as they   in unison   depart in flight
                      headed   further to
                who knows where   Sarah buys skirts and sari
                           and third eye   from India
                street market   old Lisbon   police arrest
                           drunk merchants   we drink
                espresso in sidewalk cafes   blue skies
                                   ancient bright not withered faces
                old wise faces   groceries markets restaurants
                      on every street run by
                generations and generations   fresh food fruits
                                         vegetables meats seafoods
                daily fresh   wine ports the best in the world
                      palm trees   Atlantic and
                Mediterranean breezes   it is spring
                            in Portugal   Morocco Tangier out
                the roof window   rooftops river ocean
                      spring breezes   songs   poems   dances
                the dance   Iris dances the dance of life   world
                      beat   rhythms magic alchemy
                mystery rhythms Iris dances Sarah sings
                           the poem of life   the poems of love
                Sarah and I dance love's dance in Alfama old Lisbon
                                                        in Portugal
                      from Quinta da Regaleira

to Alfama
 the water of life   oh eternal natural springs
  wash us   purify us   transform us
   sweet angel of the fountains
    of the natural springs   springs of seven mountains
     oh angel of water
      baptize us
   oh water of life
    make us new
O Privilegio dos Caminhos
 trazem a sua arte a Lisboa
  num encontro
   entre poesia canto musica e danca
Lucia Baltazar Xavier Iris Sarah Ron
                       Santiago Alquimista
 ola
  obrigado
 birth life friendship love death
   alchemy
    Sintra
  the journey below and above
Pessoa poet boulanger alchemist
poetry song dance
    the bread of life
     manger du livre   eat the book
   and the word will set you free
    changing water to red wine
     the wedding feast
      in Alfama   old Lisbon
        Iris Xavier
     our guides in this strange
      this mystical land
  Fado destiny synchronicity
    trams and church bells
     at 5am
         meditation prayer

```
                                        red wine
            Tejoo Bar
                    laughing woman
                            with a broom    Tia Aida
            Tejoo Bar    Pedro at midnight    guitared poems
                    freedom portal
                            keep the flame alive
                            the flame of freedom
            Mane    Master of Ceremonies
        Pedro sings and drinks and recites poetry
                            every night at The Tejoo Bar
            Baltazaar    Dazkarieh
                    world music   world rhythms
                            the beauty
                                of rhythmic movement of sound
        measuring space with time with magically rhythmed time
            romantic   alchemical   mystery   Portugal
                            Napoleao
                    the best wine port shop in Lisbon
                            Baixa    Rua dos Fanqueiros
                                    (tell the owner I sent you)
    in Kentucky    it's raining    Portuguese poems
            the food    the wine    the coffee    the port
                                my God oh Great Spirit
                                        i'm in Heaven
            Pasteis de Belem    Piriquita
        the French gypsy violinist    Xavier    plays and sings till dawn
                            The Friends        new friends
                    Threshold of The Gods
                        Jesus crowns Mary Magdalene
                            Ron crowns Sarah Elizabeth
                                Quinta da Regaleira
                                    Sintra
                            Fount of Abundance
                                alchemical Portugal
                                    the threshold
```

                                  the doorway
                      to the creative imagination
                      to spirit realms
      Lord Byron's Café
        Pessoa's Hotel
            by plane and train we travel
                              we walk
from Oporto to Braga Bom Jesus
     the Azores   Sintra
            to old Lisboa   Alfama
              to Faro   to Tangier
                to Terceira
Luis Vaz de Camoes   Fernando Pessoa
      Ana Paula Inacio   Luis Quintas Rui Coias
              Fado   Amalia Rodrigues
    old Lisboa   oh Lisbon   oh Portugal
              we sing your songs
                we drink your wines
                  we make love to you
                    we raise toasts to you
                      we dance your dances
                          we whisper your poems
    obrigado obrigado obrigado
                      obrigado
                            ola

10
The Wanderer

Ron & Gregory Corso, annual Jack Kerouac Festival, Lowell, Massachusetts 1993

Riding With Rebel Jesus, The Wanderer

holed up in Oaxaca we'd reached the end of the line
the government was against us an army waited for us outside
Jesus wasn't nervous he never was but neither was I
holed up in Oaxaca we'd reached the end of the line

Jesus was a wanderer wherever it was we'd been there a time or two
Bogota Buenos Aires Rio de Janeiro Machupicchu in Peru
Tucson Arizona New Orleans Louisiana Havana Cuba Mexico City
Jesus was a wanderer wherever it was we'd been there a time or two

riding with rebel Jesus people turned their heads and stared
who was that they asked did you see his eyes did you see his hair
Jesus the wanderer was a mystery to all
Jesus the wanderer was a mystery to me
riding with rebel Jesus people turned their heads and stared

how much longer can we hold out how much further can we go
we're holed up in Oaxaca with the army outside our door
looks like the journey's over our wandering days are done
how much longer can we hold out how much further can we run

holed up in Oaxaca we'd reached the end of the line
the government was against us an army waited for us outside
Jesus wasn't nervous he never was but neither was I
holed up in Oaxaca we'd reached the end of our time

11
bonus track

Hunter S. Thompson, Rani, & Ron reading "He Was A Crook"
Owl Farm, Woody Creek, Colorado, 1995

William McKeen interviews **Ron Whitehead** for

Citizen Gonzo: Hunter S. Thompson and The American Dream
(working title, subject to change)

by **William McKeen**

W. W. Norton (publisher)
release date, 2008

WM: Could you tell me about meeting Hunter and the influence he had on you?

RW: HELL'S ANGELS and FEAR and LOATHING IN LAS VEGAS and "The Kentucky Derby is Decadent and Depraved" blew my ass away. The audacity the honesty the balls the courage the brilliant brilliant writing shook me up as only a handful of poets and writers have shaken me. Rumi, William Blake, W. B. Yeats, Allen Ginsberg, Lawrence Ferlinghetti, Gregory Corso, Amiri Baraka, Bob Dylan, Knut Hamsun, Hermann Hesse, John Steinbeck, Jack Kerouac, Woody Guthrie, Hank Williams, Patsy Cline, Edvard Munch, Sarah Elizabeth, Frank Messina, Elie Wiesel, Leonard Cohen, David Amram, Johnny Depp, Bill Monroe, Loretta Lynn, Robert Penn Warren, Abraham Lincoln, Muhammad Ali, Daddy, The Dalai Lama, Gandhi, Jesus, Buddha, Mother Teresa, The Beatles, The Rolling Stones, The Clash, Martin Luther King Jr., James Joyce, T. S. Eliot, Ingmar Bergman, Al Pacino, Thomas Merton, Khalil Gibran, Edgar Cayce, Ezekiel, the British Romantic poets, the American Beat Generation, Chief Joseph, Sitting Bull, Chief Looking Horse, St. Francis of Assisi, Johnny Cash, The Carter Family, Muddy Waters, The Montgomery Brothers, Brother Matthew's Gospel Quartet, Grandaddy, John Prine, Mama, Kentucky, Hunter S. Thompson. These, and a few others. Major impacts on my life my work. Catalysts all.

I sold Hunter's work at For Madmen Only and The Store, the underground bookstore and headshop, next door to each other, on

South Limestone, Lexington Kentucky. My friend Gene Williams and I owned and operated. Late 60s early 70s. A normal day was coming in round noon, taking a hit of speed or mescaline, occasionally acid, drinking a fifth of Southern Comfort, and having a damn good time. For Madmen Only (I borrowed from Hermann Hesse's Magic Theatre in STEPPENWOLF) and The Store. Kentucky's first, certainly one of the first, and only, underground bookstore and headshop. Carried ROLLING STONE magazine from the first issue on. We carried everything. You name it we carried it. Had no idea then that I'd one day meet and work with my heroes.

I had several close encounters with Hunter. May 1995 everything changed. I've produced over 1,000 music and poetry events throughout the usa and europe including the infamous INSOMNIACATHONs. In 1994 I produced four 24 and 48 and 72 hour non-stop Music & Poetry INSOMNIACATHONs. New York University asked me to produce a 48-hour INSOMNIACATHON to kickoff their week long 50-year celebration of The Beat Generation. In 1995 I was invited back to NYU to participate in their Jack Kerouac Conference. After a packed Loeb Student Center panel discussion I stood beside Hunter as people filed up to present him with pills and joints. He pocketed the joints, turned his handfull of pills up to his mouth, emptied them there, and washed them down with his favorite drink, Chevas. Good lord! Will he survive? I was sure he would. But I wasn't sure if I wanted to be with him once all those pills kicked in. I knew then that yes by god he was a pure blooded and bloodied Kentucky boy. Kentucky is unlike any other place on planet earth. In Kentucky heroes are born. In Kentucky diamonds are created. Cause of the intense pressure from all sides. In Kentucky always I go too far. Hunter did too. He went so far he was gone. In Kentucky I pass fast on one lane bridges. In Kentucky my skin turns blue & I holler. In Kentucky smoke the grass sip the woman. In Kentucky I take deadly risks daily. In Kentucky I won't live much longer. In Kentucky I feel like I'm finally dyin. In Kentucky my mom is a prisoner. So was Hunter's mom, Virginia. I was honored to get to know her, to be her friend. Hunter asked me to visit her to check up on her. She asked me to bring her a bottle of whiskey, bourbon, whenever I visited. I did. Deborah Fuller told me that far as she could tell the last thing Virginia read before she died was a letter from me. Virginia loved Hunter. She talked about him non-stop. When our visits started she always preluded with "Okay, I'm not gonna talk about Hunter today." Then for two or three hours she talked non-stop about Hunter. She'd catch herself occasionally and say, "Ha. I said I wasn't going to talk about him and he's all I've been talking about." Then she'd have another drink and continue talking about Hunter. Visiting with Virginia was like visiting with Hunter. What a strong woman. Powerful. Smart. And, like my dad, like Hunter, well hellfire yes like me, Virginia was a 10th degree smartass. And I just happen to love smartasses. So we made damn good company. We had high energy passioned laughing our asses off visits conversations. Virginia was a good woman. A strong woman. In Kentucky moon shines comets are loud. In Kentucky music is mountainous. It's in our blood. The Cherokee, the Irish, the Scots brought music to us, shot it into our veins. We are a musical a music loving people. Even those Kentuckians who can't sing, play, or dance well they too are riddled fiddled with music.In Kentucky my life travels round the world. Hunter too. In Kentucky I am no more. Hunter too. What influence did Hunter have on me? As a child I discovered the same truth Hunter discovered as a child. Not only do we have to fight for the right to party we've got to fight for the right to be ourselves our true original creative fire perpetually burning selves. Kentuckians have certain easily identifiable traits characteristics. Independence. Honesty. Creativity. Passion. We have direct linkage via the creative imagination to the spirit realms. Genuine pure blooded Kentuckians are not religious. They are spiritual. Spiritual warriors. We will not bow down to anyone. We will stand shoulder to shoulder with other warriors who fight against injustice. We don't kiss ass. Unless we're in love. We don't look up to or down at anyone, regardless of anything. We see and treat all beings as equal. And we have issues with folks who see it otherwise, especially if they think we should do their bidding for no good reason. We believe in live and let live. Far as we're concerned the best government is the government of individual responsibility. Learn to stand on your own two feet. Help your neighbor. But don't take no shit off nobody. Although we are basically a peaceful people ain't nobody gonna capture us without a fight. There will be no hostage taking here.

Bodies on the field. We know that once somebody's tied up it's all over. We are warriors. Don't tread on me. Don't fuck with me. We're friendly people. Good people. Good neighbors. We honor and respect nature and people. But nobody gonna fuck with us. I immediately recognized all this in Hunter. He recognized it in me. We were and are friends, equals. We will always be in the trenches together. Nobody gonna fuck with us without a fight. Nobody. They may kill us. But they ain't gonna fuck with us. I don't care who they are. Amen.

WM: Could you tell me about your first trip to Owl Farm and what you observed about the way Hunter wrote/worked? (It always struck me as funny - since most of us prefer solitude for our work - that he seemed to thrive with an audience present.)

en route to Owl Farm

borrowed car
borrowed time
no insurance

Ron Whitehead

RW: June 1995. Back from NYU Kerouac Conference and several other northeast shows. I had huge exhibit set up at downtown main branch of Louisville Free Public Library. Same library where Hunter's Mom, Virginia, worked as librarian. She worked there for years, supporting her boys. Library Director told me they'd never experienced such a turnout for an exhibit. It was my biggest exhibit to date. Hundreds of signed posters, books, chapbooks, letters, recordings. My work and work I'd produced. Saturday morning. 9am. I drove to downtown post office to pick up my mail. I had one of the biggest boxes. Receiving so much mail from round world. Walking in I looked up to the big wall which included my mailbox. All the way across the wall someone had inscribed, in blood, in giant letters,
RON WHITEHEAD WILL DIE ON AUGUST 21, 1995!!!!! I stared at

the words the blood sign the death threat. I opened my mailbox. It was full. The largest package was from Allen Ginsberg. It was a work of art. Allen had used crayons to turn the entire outside of the package into a beautiful artwork. Ha! I was always excited to receive packages letters from any and all members of The Beat Generation. Warmed my heart. Inspired me. Then I remembered the death threat. Looked at it again. Stared at it. Then I drove home. Called my wife. Told her what I saw on the post office wall. She said "Go back there right now and tell someone!" I did. Within ten minutes 30 police and police dogs and the U. S. Postal Inspector, just back from Russia, were swarming the downtown Louisville post office, taking pictures, asking me at least 101 questions. One of the many items in my mail that morning was a tube package. The U. S. Postal Inspector, it turns out, was one of America's main Inspectors, an Inspector General. Hm. He was just in Russia doing what? He was concerned that the Unibomber might have sent something to me. I was interrogated. "Do you have any enemies? In the post office or otherwise." Ha. Well if you are a public figure, if you create anything at all, if you are outspoken you are always gonna have enemies. I have enemies (someone recently destroyed our webite. Homeland Security?). The FBI has had a file on me since my SDS Anti-Vietnam War activities in the 60s. Then. Everything after that. My work against injustice, US and otherwise. The U. S. Postal Inspector said they'd investigate that most likely the blood death threat had been left by someone working at the post office. He said he'd stay in touch with me, that he'd have more questions. That night, late, and nights and days to come after, the phone rang but when I, or any member of my family, answered the caller hung up. At night, for weeks, a car, cars, stopped in front of our house, doors opened and closed, then the car(s) took off always burning rubber squealing tires fleeing into the dark. What the hell was going on. Monday morning, after the Saturday morning post office death threat, I walked into the library's long gallery to check, as I did every morning, on the exhibit, to straighten up to make sure everything was still there still where it was supposed to be. I was astonished to see that someone had defaced the "Never Give Up" message/poem poster I wrote with His Holiness The Dalai Lama. Someone had scrawled "Get The Fuck Out of America! We Don't Want

You Scum Here! You Will Die!!!" Good Lord. I couldn't believe it. What was going on. I called the U. S. Postal Inspector. He had asked me to call him if anything else happened. We called back and forth several times until he finally said "Look, I'm turning this over to the F.B.I." I asked him who I should contact there. For my family's safety more than my own, I was concerned about the death threat. Over the next month, summer 1995, I had three conversations with three different F.B.I. agents trying to get some kind of information. After continued middle of the night phone call hangups and slamming car doors and screeching tires I called the F.B.I. one more time. On this my fourth call I was told "We're sorry Mr. Whitehead but your file has been lost. We've been asked to tell you to please not call again. If we find your file we'll call you." Oh my. Yes as always I was on my own. Why had I ever wasted my time by letting the post office know about the blood death threat smeared all over their downtown branch wall. Why had I even once talked with the F.B.I. I already knew their history. I made a decision. For the safety of my family we'd take a trip out west. For two weeks, during the time of my planned murder, we'd drive 5,000 miles. We'd visit Hunter S. Thompson and Lawrence Ferlinghetti. We'd visit National Parks, and more. We'd by gods go on a road trip vacation adventure. Then Mamaw died. Mamaw, mother of 13 children, including Mama, my Mama, the oldest of the 13. We packed the rental car. As soon as Mamaw's funeral was over we headed west. Life. Death. Love. Family. Threats. Murder.
After Pike's Peak we made it to Independence Pass then entered Aspen the back way. By the time we found Woody Creek then Owl Farm it was dark. As we got out of the car the sound of a bear killing and eating what sounded like a baby blasted, via loudspeakers, across the yards out into the fields and the woods and no doubt all the way down to Woody Creek Tavern to the people sitting outside eating and drinking all of them wondering what in hell's going on up Hunter's way. I'd already told my kids, Nathanial, Rani, Dylan, bout Hunter. Hell, they'd grown up with me as their Dad. They didn't bat an eye. We knocked on the door. Deborah Fuller answered with a smile and an open armed "come on in." Hunter knew I was coming. I'd called midday crossing beautiful Colorado back country. He was up. He had just gotten up. Up

all night. Sleep all day. Routine. Fruit juice. Healthy breakfast, right after sundown, prepared by Deborah. Bloody Mary. Chevas. Smoke. Snort. Drink. Mixture of this and that and that and this. Everything necessary. Loaded guns. Alcohol. Drugs. "I never recommend alcohol and drugs to anyone but they always work for me." A man. A real man. A Kentucky man. Pure blood. Mutant pure blood. Mixed blood. Mut. Roughneck. Genius. Madman. Southern Gentleman. Only through the doors of excess can we ever know enlightenment. Wake Up! be Buddha. Awake. The test. Smoke some weed. Share the pipe. A little later. The wooden bowl. White powder. Cocaine. I've smoked a lot of pot but never been huge fan. But I love cocaine. I've never been a downer barbituate person. Shit. Life is too damn slow already. Why do I want to slow it down anymore. I want to speed it up. Speed amphetamines cocaine mescaline peyote lsd ecstasy. Speed it up. Life. Ecstasy. Too much agony. Give me ecstasy. Altered states. Be the bridge tween matter and spirit. Joy. Happiness. The Dalai Lama looked into my eyes and said, "It's okay to be happy." Then he laughed, real loud. An awakening moment for me. Same as meeting Hunter. The Dalai Lama and Hunter. One and the same. Both Masters. Teachers. Catalysts. Transformers. Lightning Bolts. Both. Hunter offered me cocaine. Man oh man I wanted some. But I told him that since my family was with me I'd pass.

I had Published in Heaven posters for Hunter to sign. His Nixon "He Was A Crook" obituary. We had wonderful visit. Hunter loved Ferlinghetti. He signed poster for him. We talked bout Ferlinghetti and all The Beats, our association with them. He said he'd always thought he was a good shot til he went shooting with Bill Burroughs. Ha. Hunter asked me to read the "He Was A Crook" poster to him. I did. (photo of Ron reading poster to Hunter) He said when Nixon died everyone was praising him, everyone cept Hunter. He said only person who publically praised his Nixon obituary was Sargent Shriver. Hunter said "I'm gonna sign one of these to Sargent Shriver and I want you to get it to him okay." I said "okay" and he started signing. He signed with gold and silver markers. The marker he was using jammed. He went berserk. He started screaming "FUCK FUCK FUCK WHAT'S

WRONG WITH THIS GODDAMN THING DOESN'T ANYTHING WORK ANYMORE FUCK FUCK FUCK!!!!" and on. Deborah Fuller rushed over. She got behind him. Draped her arms over his shoulders onto his chest and in calming soothing voice said "It's okay everything's okay Hunter it's okay Hunter calm down relax reelax it's okay Hunter" and on until gradually Hunter calmed back down. He took another marker out of a drawer, a drawer which was full of gold and silver markers, and finished signing the poster personalizing it to Sargent Shriver. Later, after returning to Kentucky, I sent the poster to Sargent Shriver. He was deeply appreciative of it. We corresponded for a while. He thought the world of Hunter, thought Hunter was a true fearless American hero. Hunter had passages from POLO IS MY LIFE tacked all over a wall. Games were on the tv. Hunter would bet on a frog race. Jack Nicholson called three times while we were there. Hunter always had the speaker phone, his main hotline phone, on. Jack had flown out to Aspen to get away for the weekend and to watch heavyweight fight with Hunter. Hunter didn't know Jack had brought his daughters with him. Hunter snuck up to Jack's house, broke a window, and through hundreds of firecrackers in scaring hell outta Jack's daughters. Jack at first was giving Hunter hell. Then by third call Jack was saying everything was okay that me and the girls all love you Hunter. Ha. We shared gifts with Hunter he with us. Hugs all round. Hunter loved people. He loved children, families. He loved his son, Juan. Hunter was a southern gentleman and a genius madman a prophet a messenger a shaman. One of The Best Damn Writers of all time, bar none. We traveled on into the dark night through Colorado to Utah Nevada California. We had an awesome visit with my friend Lawrence Ferlinghetti. We visited several National Parks before winding our way back to Kentucky. Hunter had asked me to visit and watch out for his Mom, Virginia. Soon as we arrived back to Kentucky I called Virginia, picked up bottle of whiskey, went to visit her then returned home took a nap then drove to Boston and Cambridge where I met The Dalai Lama then I drove back to Kentucky took a nap then drove back to New York City JFK airport parked my rental car in long term parking then headed to my first reading tour of The Netherlands. whew. This was my regular schedule for years and years! How did I survive. How did Hunter. Guardian angels. Strong will. Keep on keepin on. Never Give Up. But when the time comes to go. Go. No regrets no surrender.

WM: What role did you play in the Louisville Tribute and what are your strongest recollections of that visit?

RW: I produced The Official Hunter S. Thompson Tribute. March 1996. Freedom Hall. Louisville, Kentucky. Coaching Dylan's 13-year old team in big annual tournament. Dylan, my youngest of three children. We won the first two games. The first against a big team which included an almost seven footer who went on to star at the University of Louisville. We've got a damn good team. But this third game is something else. Playing biggest bunch of rednecks I've seen in a while. Cheating abounds. Other team's parents are cussing our kids ("you little fuckers!") plus they're yelling calling me every name in the book ridiculing my long hair and my goatee. I ignore them completely. Questionable call after questionable call. The game is stopped several times cause of arguing pushing shoving name calling. We get beat by one point. My players are so mad they rapidly exit the court. I turn to track them down and tell them to get their asses back out here and shake hands with the other team. I'm as fierce a competitor as you'll ever meet. But I always remember that it's a game. Play the game at 110mph giving life blood fully immersed in it but never forget that it's a game. Be a fierce but compassionate warrior. Be a good sport. After the game shake hands, regardless of the outcome. Soon as I turn to chase down my players I'm faced by a brute force army of parents, parents of the opposing team, the team that had just cheated and won the game by one point. A man my height, 6'1", but weighing in 100 pounds heavier, gets in my face and says "You starin at her?!" Even though I'd heard every word these idiots had yelled at my players and me I hadn't once acknowledged their presence. And that had infuriated them. When Brute asked me the question in an instant I thought hm is there a woman in this group of redneck parent assholes who I should've been lookin at. I took a quick glance round the dozen women. Nope. All of them were uglier than the ugliest damn chicken in the barnyard. I looked back at this idiot, stared him straight in the eyes, smiled and said

"No." He said "You laughin at me?!" I knew then that dumbass just wanted to show off to his little clan wanted to show them what a man what a bad boy he thought he was. I turned to go after my boys. Next thing I knew I was coming to, on the floor, everything spinning. I got sucker punched. I've been hit many times, playing sports, by my Dad, in fights. But I'd never been hit like this. I touched my face. My nose was flat resting over on my right cheek. The left side of my face was sunk in. Being a fan of martial arts revenge and action movies and books I immediately thought that I may have just received a death blow and might only have seconds or minutes to live. I knew that at least my nose and jaw were broken. I attempted to get someone's anyone's attention. Finally a person then people then the police came. One of our mother's, a vice-president of National City bank, grabbed her 6-year old son, and ran after the guy who sucker punched me. Running through Freedom Hall she yelled "Somebody stop him! He hit our coach!" A man took up the chase and was able to write down the sucker puncher's license plate number as he raced out of the Freedom Hall parking lot. I was rushed to the hospital. I had a broken nose, jaw, cheek, a permanently dislocated jaw, and a concussion. It took two surgeries to straighten my face up. I wore wires in my mouth for three years. A great deal of cosmetic surgery had to be done in my mouth to get it back to a semblance of normal. I was teaching at the University of Louisville. Fortunately my boss, Joe Slavin, the best teacher in the history of teaching, allowed me to abbreviate my teaching schedule for the remainder of the spring '96 semester. I spent weeks on our broke down couch, barely able to move. My vision too had been damaged. I needed dark. When I went out I wore sunglasses. Three days after being hit the police arrested the guy. I've never filed charges against anyone but I didn't want my kids to think that it was okay, in an already rampantly violent culture, to hit and nearly kill someone just cause you wanted to show off for some women. The brute told the police that the only reason he hit me was to defend himself, that he was afraid I was going to hurt him. He got off with one year of public service at Secret Heart Academy, a catholic high school for young women. He had to pay my medical expenses but I still ended up with nearly $15,000 in dental bills. My wife, Sarah, and I have payed that debt down to

$5,000. We continue to make monthly payments. Douglas Brinkley, the person directly responsible for resurrecting Hunter S. Thompson's writing career, and editor of Hunter's brilliant letters, Douglas Brinkley and I had already agreed to produce INSOMNIACATHON 1996 NEW ORLEANS in August. I had been working on it for three months. I was determined that this unexpected physical calamity would not keep me from making this INSOMNIACATHON happen. I summoned up my will power doing everything I could to get back on my feet, finish my semester of teaching, meet all the commitments I'd already made to present readings of my own work, and to produce INSOMNIACATHON 1996 NEW ORLEANS. In May and June I started taking driving and flying trips to New Orleans, getting the ball rolling, making all the contacts, setting everything up. Doug knows as many people as I do so he too was making contacts. We decided to get a historic marker placed in front of the Algiers home of William S. Burroughs, the house Burroughs lived in for a time, a time mentioned in Jack Kerouac's ON THE ROAD, a time during which Burroughs was arrested. I did a long, and difficult, interview with Burroughs discussing this period of his life. After that interview I swore I'd never interview anyone else. I thought the world of Burroughs, and totally respected his work. But interviewing him was like pulling my own teeth, it wasn't easy. We held the 48-hour non-stop Music & Poetry INSOMNIACATHON at The New Orleans Contemporary Arts Center, The Howlin' Wolf Club, and The Mermaid Lounge. August 16-18, 1996. One of the best damn events I'm proud to say I produced. It was an amazing amazing experience, beginning to end. Doug and I brought in Amiri Baraka, George McGovern, Amy Carter, Robert Creeley, Jay McInerney, John Rechy, Andrei Codrescu, David Amram, Christopher Felver, Diane DiPrima, Lawrence Ferlinghetti, Ramblin' Jack Elliott, Richard Hell, E. Ethelbert Miller, Edward Sanders, Robert Palmer, John Sinclair, tom Piazza, The Iguanas, The Wild Magnolias, Frank Messina, Casey Cyr, Nicole Blackman, Louis Bickett, Hersch Silvermann, James Grauerholz, William S. Burroughs (live phone conversation) and so many other poets writers musicians and artists plus Doug and I gave talks and read and mced hosted the entire 48-hour non-stop event. I was Guest Editor for TRIBE magazine which at the time was New Orleans' main cultural magazine. The issue right before our special INSOMNIACATHON issue featured Jim Jarmusch. We had art exhibits and films. Thousands of people came from all over the country. National and international news media covered it. The TIMES PICAYUNE named it New Orleans' Best New Event of 1996. We had an after party at Doug's condo. That's when I told Doug about my idea to produce an Official Hunter S. Thompson Tribute in Hunter's hometown of Louisville, Kentucky. Nobody in Louisville or Kentucky had paid any real tribute to Hunter. Doug loved the idea and said Hunter will too. The conversations began. Phone calls, faxes, visits. We agreed on a date, December 12th, 1996. Hunter wanted to have the event at Memorial Auditorium on 4th Street, downtown Louisville, a few blocks from the main library where his Mom, Virginia, had worked for years. Back in the day, for a time, Memorial Auditorium had been the main place for big events for concerts. I reserved the venue. I got the University of Louisville to come on board as co-sponsor, basically footing the bill. I'd to all the production work, UofL would cover any expenses that weren't met through ticket sales. September 1996. I was still in terrible physical condition from being hit. Surgeries, orthodontists, mouth wired, severe nauseating migraine headaches, blurred vision. I was back to doing readings. The wires cut my mouth and I spit blood on the pages as I read. Blood of the poet. My wore out copy of Hozomeen Press' I WILL NOT BOW DOWN still has the stains to prove. Hozomeen Press, Connecticut Rhode Island New York. I did so much with them. Rich Martin, Casey Cyr, Denis Mahoney. Beautiful people. Black Pig Liberation Front. My friend Lee Ranaldo, Sonic Youth, hooked us up. I have done so much work with all of them and hope to continue doing so. I was back to teaching at UofL, producing events, publishing, branching out to throughout europe and the usa. Traveling more and more. Busier than ever. Synchronicity brought Kentuckian Johnny Depp into the picture. He was staying with Hunter for a few months, studying him in order to be him in the film version of FEAR and LOATHING in LAS VEGAS, one of Hunter's masterpieces. Johnny is one of the greatest actors of all time. A true artist. A genuine person. A damn good guy. A nice guy, a gentleman, but, as a true Kentuckian, somebody you don't want to fuck with. I brought together an army of young people to help me with the event. I assigned Section Leaders. Ashley Farmer took care of travel. At first everyone seemed fine to fly Economy. But the closer we got to the event everybody decided that First Class was the only way to go. Ha. No problem for me, UofL would pick up any overage. J.B. Wilson contacted the Governor of Kentucky and arranged for Hunter, Johnny Depp, Warren Zevon, Douglas Brinkley, David Amram, and myself to be named Kentucky Colonels and given full privileges accordingly. Ha. We got Louisville Mayor Jerry Abramson to officially designate December 12, 1996 as Hunter S. Thompson Day. A delegate from the Mayor's office attended the event presenting me with The Key and the certificate which I presented to Hunter. Ok. I lined up an allstar cast for The Official Hunter S. Thompson Tribute: Hunter, his Mom Virginia, his son Juan, Hunter's bodyguard Sheriff of Pitkin County, Johnny Depp, Warren Zevon, Douglas Brinkley, Roxanne Pulitzer, Harry Dean Stanton (got pneumonia called but regrettably couldn't make it but wanted to real bad), Laila Nabulsi, David Amram, Harvey Sloane, Susi Wood, Annie McClanahan, New Horizon, & others. I read and hosted the event. A & E, Arts & Entertainment, Stephen Land filmed the event as did Wayne Ewing. The Courier-Journal (Kentucky's New York Times), LEO (Louisville alternative), and Lexington's Herald-Leader all ran features. The event was covered by national and international media. The New York Times gave it a rave review. My army of young people and I lined everything up. This was a major event. It was beyond a big job. Hunter wanted control of every aspect of it. He became more and more nervous. Absolutely no one from his hometown his home state had paid him any serious respects tributes nobody had honored him the way I knew he should have been honored. And by gods come hell or high water I was gonna do. Then UofL, one week before the event, fearing adverse negative publicity, backed out on me. I was struggling with my health. I was working around the clock, which i've done most of my life. I was in well way beyond pathetic financial situation. Although I had broken even, or made or lost a little, on the hundreds of music and poetry events i'd produced well a few yes there had been a few like for example the 1994 NYU INSOMNIACATHON i'd lost money on. The NYU INSOMNIACATHON burnt my ass up to the tune of $20,000. in the hole. At the end of that event i thought about jumping off the roof of the NYU student center. But somehow i'd figured it out. Well kind of. For six months after returning from NYU INSOMNIACATHON my family and i had no electricity no lights no hot water. for six months. so I didn't quite figure it out. But i had eventually gotten back on my feet. During those six months I continued to find ways to produce events to publish to teach to write. But I was running deep in debt from supporting the arts. Carrying a $20-30,000 debt. Juggling. Walking tight wire. Now UofL backs out as co-sponsor of The Official Hunter S. Thompson Tribute. I'd done my part. Everything was set up, ready to go. But my sponsor vanished. I'm left, yet again, holding the bag. Oh my God! What to do?! I called Doug. He said "Ron you're gonna have to suck it up. It's too late to turn back. If you follow through with this it'll be one of the biggest events of alltime and certainly the biggest in Hunter's life. You've got to do this Ron. If you do you'll truly prove to the world what you're made of." whew. I sucked it up. with some help. two of my best friends, my doctor and longtime friend Dr. Nanine Henderson and poet friend Bill Smith, came through for me by paying for airfares and hotel bills. But even with their help I ended up getting stuck with $50,000 in debts. The event cost $100,000. Via ticket and product sales we made $50,000. Sarah and I are still, eleven years after the event, making payments on balance of $6,000. Everyone was in town for several days. Hunter wanted to stay at The Brown Hotel. The Brown and The Seelbach were Louisville's most historic and finest hotels. I put Johnny Depp and Warren Zevon and others up at The Brown, all under aliases. I put David Amram and others up at The Seelbach. There was a fight amongst many young woman to determine who was gonna ride to the airport with me to pick up Johnny Depp and his two associates who were flying in on Johnny's private jet. The first thing Johnny said when he set foot on the ground, at the airport, was "Damn it feels good to be home!" He was carrying his guitar over his shoulder. good trip from airport to hotel. talked bout Kentucky. Johnny and I both born in Owensboro, western Kentucky. talked about our families. bout Hollywood and how he ready to find another place to live. we had several talks during his visit. bout his brother, his reading, his writing.

he asked if i'd edit some of his work. said i'd be glad to. Johnny's a good person. and genius actor. I had limo for Hunter. and small fleet of Lincoln Continentals. all of which he requested. he said "look i know you're strapped for money i know bout UofL backing out but i need for you to bring me $3,000 in cash in $20 bills in a brown paper bag. knock on the door. i'll stick my hand through and you hand it to me. that's how we'll start. then i need two young attractive women to be my assistants for the entire time (several days). after you deliver the cash in the brown paper bag i'll need the limo, and limo driver, ready to go. i have things to do places to go people to meet." i said "okay." two wild sexy young ladies students of mine jumped at the opportunity to be Hunter's personal assistants for the duration of his visit. after delivery of the cash Hunter's first stop was Leatherhead on Bardstown Road. the owners, Nick and Lynn, are friends. Nick is world class master leather artist. Hunter bought 3 whips, same as Churchill Downs jockeys use on their horses. before the limo pulled away one of the young ladies ran across the street to Twice Told Coffeehouse to show her boyfriend, who was working the counter, her new boots that Hunter S. Thompson had just bought her. Story goes that she also described exactly what she did to be granted such a gift. Pretty sure the relationship ended there at the counter of Twice Told. Hunter didn't sleep for days and nights. He got more and more nervous tense anxious anxiety ridden. He visited old friends male and female visited old girlfriends. Several times everyone gathered in his hotel room where he held court. He brought gifts for me, and others. While stressed he was simultaneously happy. Like a boy at Christmas. He was home. and finally finally he was receiving long overdue respect. Hunter and i had several long talks about the event and about our lives. There was partying merriment. non-stop. days and nights of it. i was beyond stressed out coordinating this gigantic HST-Day military campaign. General Whitehead what about this what about that etc. the entire time seeing the other end the after the tribute and what i was gonna have to do to clean up the mess but i was also focussed on making sure everything going smooth no problems that everyone has exactly what they want what they need making sure Hunter makes it to the show cause he, like George Jones, was known for the no-show hell i had friends who sometimes got so fucked up that they weren't able to make it to their own performances and so i sure as hell didn't want that to happen here so yes i was on pins and needles no i was on nails and spikes. but i was raised by the toughest of the tough, my Dad, so i'd learned how to keep it together in the midst of the battle no matter how severe how bloody the battle. and i did. i kept it together. Memorial Auditorium filled up. to capacity and beyond. SRO. Hunter's limo driver said something Hunter considered improper and Hunter flogged him with his whip. the driver shut the hell up and drove. Hunter was supposed to arrive from The Brown to Memorial Auditorium early. his Mom wanted to visit with him. He was nervous about visiting with his Mom. Hunter was 15 minutes late. my wife, with a driver in one of our fleet of Lincoln Continentals, had picked Virginia up from the Episcopal home, the nicest of retirement homes, where Hunter and his brother had ensconced her. She liked the place. she said tho that "some of these damn old people walk in here and start talking with me and then i finally realize they've got Alzheimer's and they don't know their ass from a hole in the ground or who they are or who i am and it's gotten to where it pisses me off they're sposed to be kept in a separate wing but they get out and wander everywhere including into my room dammit." Virginia was there, sitting up close. Hunter's son Juan had been there the entire time. I'd asked Juan to write a tribute piece for his Dad. He did. he asked me to edit it. I did. it was beautiful. being father of 3, i knew it would tear Hunter up. and it did. right before it was Juan's turn to go on stage and read he came to me and said "Ron i've got to talk with you." we went to back corner of stage. he said "Ron i just don't believe i can do this. i'm nervous." i grabbed his shoulders looked into his eyes and said "Juan your tribute piece will be the most precious part of the night it will mean more to your Dad than anything anyone else says. you've got to read it. you have no choice." he said "okay." he did and what a job he did. it tore everybody up including Hunter who i was standing beside and i saw Hunter get choked up and wipe tears away and then try and act like nothing was going on that he wasn't emotional. Hunter was 30 minutes late. Hunter was 60 minutes late. the natives were definitely restless. i gave them updates. trying to calm them down. i read them a couple of wildass pieces to work them up. ha. Hunter was an hour and a half late. then then then the limo was spotted circling Memorial Auditorium. one pass. two. it pulled up to the back entrance, by the dressing rooms, the green rooms, the green rooms into which Hunter had demanded live circuit tv be added. good lord. the bills running up higher and higher. then Roxanne Pulitzer and the guy she was with arrived and oh my oh my yes she did a fantastic job reading paying tribute to Hunter on stage but backstage she was pure spoiled prima donna brat. i avoided her. believe me i was in no mood to listen to that shit. i didn't care if she read or not. i announced to audience that Hunter was In The House!!! the place went nuts. lights went down. spotlight came up. on Warren Zevon kickin ass on Lawyers Guns and Money. oh my. we were all. well over 2,000 of us in heaven. the show lasted 3 hours. Hunter's best childhood friends spoke. Warren Zevon sang songs he said Hunter had inspired. he said Hunter had made him a millionaire. God Bless Warren! what a sweet angry rebel genius. one of the best songwriters! i'd asked David Amram to be music maestro conductor for the evening. what an amazing job he did!!! plus he performed his own work including a special tribute he wrote for Hunter. Annie McClanahan, daughter of Ed McClanahan and Cia White, read two poems. Hunter loved her. She hung out with the entire wild crowd after the show until somewhere in the wee hours 3 or 4 or 5am sunday morning Hunter drove her in one of yes one of the fleet of Lincoln Continentals drove Annie in reverse backing up at high speeds through yards and all over Cherokee Road til he deposited her at her Mom's door. praise the lord. i don't know how. yes i do. guardian angels protected us all. otherwise there would've been bodies broken bodies broken vehicles broken homes. there certainly were broken relationships. folk singer Susi Wood and one of the best bluegrass bands on the planet which included Steve Cooley and Jimmy Brown (Guitar Emporium) and man i wish i could remember the other names well they tore it up. former Louisville Mayor Harvey Sloane gave remembrance and read from HELL'S ANGELS. Sheriff of Pitkin County told about Hunter's run for sheriff he being a Hunter supporter when Hunter lost by slimmest of margins decided to run himself and won and became Hunter protector. Doug Brinkley presented eloquent erudite talk and i am thankful to Brinkley for resurrecting Hunter's career transporting it to new audiences and gaining Hunter respect he so richly deserves including having his masterpieces included with the Classics of all literature. earlier in evening i read Gimme Back My Wig: The Hound Dog Taylor Hunter S. Thompson Blues. the place erupted, went nuts. Hunter asked me to read Nixon obituary He Was A Crook but he in back room watching on film kept yelling for me to "slow down" that i was reading too fast but i was yes reading at same pace i read it to him at Owl Farm which he loved so i knew it was stress no sleep drugs alcohol Hunter kept sending Tammy out to ask me to "slow down" but i didn't so Hunter kept cussing and screaming in back room Johnny said "calm down Hunter Ron's a passionate man" finally Hunter brought fire extinguisher out and sprayed me. he emptied every fire extinguisher, a dozen, out that night. i had to pay to have them all refilled. a little later in program after this i had introduced David Amram and Hunter was standing behind me a foot to my left backstage was crowded with a growing number of people i dropped some of my papers notes on the floor which was wet now from folks especially Hunter spilling Chevas, wine, beer, water and more on the floor so when Hunter saw me drop my papers he immediately starting stomping them into the wetness. i had to catch myself from tackling him but no i wanted the show to go on i was determined to ride out the tornado. Billy Hardison tapped me on the shoulder telling me that Mojo Nixon was backstage and wondered if he could be included in the event. I asked Hunter, back again in his green room, and Hunter started yelling "Fuck No! I remember what he said about me!" so Mojo didn't get included. Johnny Depp read. he said later that looking back he regretted chewing gum while reading. he also fielded questions from the audience for Hunter. Johnny used flashlight to point out who got next turn. end of Tribute and what a Tribute it was everyone came on stage David Amram conductor also played flute Johnny Depp at David's side Johnny on guitar Warren Zevon on grand piano Susi Wood and bluegrass band everyone stood playing singing we'd printed copies of My Old Kentucky Home and added them to the program so everyone over 2,000 stood in Memorial Auditorium opened their hearts and joined in singing one of Hunter's alltime favorite songs My Old Kentucky Home. then it was over. Hunter said he'd sign books but he didn't. all the books had sold out. the new Random House 25th annivervary edition of FEAR & LOATHING IN LAS VEGAS. all other Hunter books sold out. all the Hunter cds had sold out. we sold many of the Hunter posters i'd produced. and event t-shirts and sweatshirts. the stage was swarmed by audience members wanting to meet Hunter and Johnny. Hunter escaped in the limo back to The Brown. Johnny hung around and visited with many, with his 2 young bodyguards at his side, then the 3 of them walked back to the Brown. some idiot snuck into Johnny's green room and set his chair on fire. we had to beat it out. the fire extinguishers were empty. i had to pay for the chair. i am eternally grateful to each and every person, and there were many, who helped me produce that unbelievably amazing event. neither A&E nor Wayne Ewing gave me film copy of the event, as they both promised. i made calls. no result. Louisville's NPR affiliate radio station had asked for permission to record the event which they did agreeing also to give me a copy. said they couldn't locate it. hm. aw well. a former student of mine Jim Gilbert did give me photos. the entire wild ride is stored right here in the most important place, my heart. i have no regrets. i'm glad i did it. if i had it to do over i'd do it. it was one of the best events i've ever produced and been associated with. and i'm especially glad i did it for Hunter. i still run into people in Louisville who consider me anathema simply because of my association with Hunter S. Thompson. yes there's much more to tell bout the Tribute. oh yes. when Hunter's Mom Virginia took it upon herself to go back stage and visit her son the first thing she did was give him hell about the outfit he had on that he should have more respect for himself and dress properly for such an occasion. God Bless Virginia! what a woman! God Bless Hunter! what a man! enuf.

WM: I have your list of suggested ways for Kentucky to honor this native son but what kind of reactions have you gotten to that?

RW: On February 22nd, 2005 I wrote "Dr. Hunter Shaman Thompson is dead, a tribute." On March 9, 2005 Sarah and I produced a tribute to Hunter at The Rudyard Kipling, a Louisville landmark. Sarah performed some of Hunter's favorite songs plus other Hunter related themed songs. I read my tribute to Hunter, read other Hunter related pieces, and told a few Hunter stories. I shared a message and blessing from Hunter's wife Anita who I had a long talk with earlier in the day. She was thankful for and moved by the fact that Hunter's friends in his hometown were remembering him via the tribute. We invited folks to read their own remembrances. I read my "13 Suggestions for Louisville, Kentucky to pay tribute to native son Hunter S. Thompson." The Rud was packed, wall to wall, the crowd flowed out the doors into the night. All ages, from teenagers to 80 and 90 year olds. People from all walks of life. We were moved inspired uplifted by the mutual gathering sharing of energies of stories poems songs each and every one dedicated to our fallen hero. Master bookbinder Amanda Buck attended the memorial happening. She, like the rest of us, was deeply moved by the event. She volunteered to do what she could to help make as many of my 13 Suggestions as possible reach fruition. I said if you're serious contact me. She did. We met at our apartment in The Highlands. I told Amanda that I had sent my Suggestions to many people but with little to no result. I said that producing The Official Hunter S. Thompson Tribute in 1996 and now the Memorial Tribute in 2005 was bout as much as i could do. That if she wanted to pick up the ball and run with it that i'd provide her with all my Hunter Tribe contacts. She enthusiastically embraced the opportunity. In the following weeks and months Amanda, consummate professional courteous friendly diplomat, worked relentlessly. Step by step, person by person, she made progress. She got permissions and permits and every detail of necessary information to place a historic marker in front of the Thompson Family Home on Ransdell Avenue, to get a Hunter Memorial Marker placed at an entrance to Cherokee Park, to get a giant photo banner of Hunter displayed on a downtown Louisville highrise, to start a Hunter collection at the University of Louisville Library, and more. She also discovered that every project was expensive and required funding, money that neither Amanda nor Sarah and I have. Amanda is now working to raise the thousands, tens of thousands, of dollars necessary to make at least several of my 13 Suggestions happen. I hope she succeeds. In my eyes she has already succeeded by accomplishing all she has. I am thankful. I am thankful to Sarah (on

September 15, 2006 Sarah & I also produced Keep Louisville Gonzo/Road to Hunter: an evening of gonzo film, music, and writing) and to others who worked tirelessly to help me pay Tribute to Hunter S. Thompson. I know Hunter is thankful too.

Ron Whitehead's 13 suggestions for Louisville, Kentucky to pay tribute to native son Hunter S. Thompson:

1) Courier-Journal (Kentucky's main daily newspaper) devote entire Saturday SCENE (arts/culture section) to Hunter's life and work. (hasn't been done)

2) LEO and Velocity (Louisville's weekly alternative newspapers) devote entire issues to Hunter's life and work. (LEO did feature on Hunter right after his death. but they haven't devoted entire issue to him)

3) WFPK 91.9fm (all music) and WFPL 89.5fm (all news) (Louisville's Public Radio Partnership, NPR affiliate) devote one week of programming to Hunter's life and work. (hasn't been done)

4) Baxter Avenue Theatres (Louisville's art film theatres) start Annual Hunter S. Thompson Film Festival. (hasn't been done)

5) Place historic marker in front of Thompson Family home on Ransdell Avenue in Louisville's Highlands neighborhood. Purchase the home and turn it into Hunter Museum similar to what Kentucky did for Bill Monroe's Rosine, Ohio County, Kentucky home. (Amanda got permission to do marker)

6) Place giant Hunter photo banner on downtown highrise, visible from Interstate 64, near new Muhammad Ali museum, same as Muhammad Ali & Pee Wee Reese banners. (Amanda got all info but costs $40-50,000 for the giant banner)

7) Rename The Louisville Free Public Library (the main library at 4th & York downtown) The Hunter and Virginia Thompson Free Public Library. Hunter's Mom Virginia retired, as librarian, from same library. Have a Hunter S. Thompson Room for students & scholars. (hasn't happened)

8) Rename Louisville's Cherokee Road Hunter S. Thompson Road. (hasn't happened)

9) Move the Daniel Boone statue (Daniel with rifle), at entrance to Cherokee Park, to Boone County. Replace it with statue of Hunter with typewriter, gun, and other necessary Hunter items. (hasn't happened)

10) Rename Cherokee Park Hunter S. Thompson Park. (hasn't happened)

11) University of Louisville start Annual Hunter S. Thompson International Literature Symposium. University of Louisville Rare Books and Archives purchase, catalogue, and exhibit Hunter's entire archives. (hasn't happened but Delinda Buie, Director of Rare Books and Archives, is ready to start collection.)

12) City of Louisville designate July 18th Annual Official Hunter S. Thompson Day, Public Holiday, No School, No Work, Concert on The Great Lawn at Ohio River Waterfront, downtown. Musicians/Bands perform their own but especially some of Hunter's favorite songs. (hasn't happened)

13) Keep Louisville Gonzo (this came to me in a dream)!

People continue to say that there will be no audience for Hunter S. Thompson's work, that no one will understand or care. Yet, as I travel across America across the world working with young people, of all ages, I witness a movement away from the constraints of non-democratic puritan totalitarian cultures, governments. I see a new generation that recognizes the lies of the power elite, a generation that is turning to the freethinkers the freedom fighters of the 50s and 60s recognizing honoring them as mentors.

I have heard more than once that Hunter S. Thompson is a madman. That oh look what he could have done if he lived a more sane sensible life. Nobel Prize winner Elie Wiesel, in THE TOWN BEYOND THE WALL, says: "Mad Moishe, the fat man who cries when he sings and laughs when he is silent...Moishe - I speak of the real Moishe, the one who hides behind the madman - is a great man. He is far-seeing. He sees worlds that remain inaccessible to us. His madness is only a wall, erected to protect us - us: to see what Moishe's bloodshot eyes see would be dangerous." In Jewish mysticism the prophet often bears the facade of madness. Hunter S. Thompson stands in direct lineage to the great writers and prophets. And as with the prophets of old, the message may be too painful for the masses to tolerate, to hear, to bear. They may, and usually do, condemn, even kill, the messenger. Hunter stood as long as he could. He fought a valiant fight. He was a brave yet sensitive soul. He was a sacred shaman warrior. He saw. He felt. He recorded his visions. He took alcohol and drugs to ease the pain generated by what he saw what he felt. He lived on his own terms. He died on his own terms. Did the masses kill Hunter? Did he kill himself? He found the courage to stand up against the power mongers and the masses. At least thirteen times he should have died but, miraculously, didn't. He chose to take his own life. He completed the work he came to do. His Termination Date arrived. He came, he saw, he conquered, he departed.

If life is a dream, as some suggest, sometimes beautiful sometimes desperate, then Hunter's work is the terrible saga of the ending of time for The American Dream. With its action set at the heart of darkness of American materialist culture, with war as perpetual background, playing on the television, Hunter S. Thompson, like the prophets of old, shows how we, through greed and powerlust, have already gone over the edge. As Jack Kerouac, through his brilliant oeuvre, breathed hope into international youth culture Thompson shows how the ruling power-elite is not about to share what it controls with idealists yearning for a world of peace love and understanding.

We must look beyond the life of the artist, no matter how interesting, to the work the body of work itself. That is the measure of success. Like those who have re-examined George Orwell's 1984 to find a multi-layered literary masterpiece, we must look deep into Hunter S. Thompson's work and find the deep multi-layered messages. His books, especially the early ones and his letters, are literary masterpieces equal to the best writing ever produced.

Knowledge, from the inception of Modernism, and through post-modernism and chaos to The Ocean of Consciousness, is reorganized, redefined through Literature, Art, Music, and Film. The genres are changing, the canons are exploding, as is culture. The mythopoetics, the privileged sense of sight, of modern, contemporary, avant-garde cutting edge Nabi poets, musicians, artists, filmmakers are examples of art forms of a society, a culture, a civilization, a world, in which humanity lives, not securely in cities nor innocently in the country, but on the apocalyptic, simultaneous edge of a new realm of being and understanding. The mythopoet, female and male, the shaman, Hunter S. Thompson returns to the role of prophet-seer by creating myths that resonate in the minds of readers, myths that speak with the authority of the ancient myths, myths that are gifts from the shadow.

the end. i thank you William for asking me for persevering and continuing to ask me to do this interview. i am grateful to you. i am glad your HST book is being published. i don't plan on doing any more interviews. too painful. i hope this is the last one.

what is language
but an experiment an adventure
a failed attempt
to communicate.
i refuse all language barriers.

Ron Whitehead, poet
The Highlands, Cherokee Park
Louisville, Kentucky
May 28, 2007, Memorial Day
AHA

GIMME BACK MY WIG
The Hound Dog Taylor Hunter S. Thompson Blues

by Ron Whitehead

Gimme Back My Wig

I Got The Hound Dog Taylor Hunter S. Thompson

                        Gimme Back My Wig

   I Gotta Get Out Of This Town   Blues

Gimme Back My Wig
   cause I'm thumbin a ride after midnight on
      The Hound Dog Taylor Alligator
   New Orleans Memphis Chicago 61 Blues Highway yes
   I gotta get out of this town fore somebody does me in

Gimme Back My Wig
   the blonde crew cut is the only one that'll work now
      cause it's already late
  maybe too late in these last days final hours of this Rush
   Limbaugh Newt Gingrich Pat Buchanan Jesse
   Helms George Bush Ronald Reagan Richard
    Nixon Joseph McCarthy J. Edgar Hoover
     Cheney Ashcroft Rumsfield Rove Bush Jr
   new age government this Pat Robertson

Jerry Falwell cult christian coalition
moral majority american renaissance
KKK neonazi militiaman takeover of
America

the Land of the Free Home of the Brave
we Killed the Indians why not the
Decadent Poets Artists Musicians
Blacks Jews Hispanics Asians
Muslims HomoLesbians Beat
Generation X Smart Women
Outsiders the Sad Downtrodden
Stepped on Walked on
Kicked and Killed
all the morally
depraved

yes please Gimme Back My Wig
I don't think the red Afro gonna work need that
skinhead look tonight slippin
left to right and over the fence outta this hellhole backstreet
underground alley I been crowded into by
American
brownshirtarmbandschoolyardBullyThugs

Gimme Back My Wig
I'm climbing out the back window paint brushes and pens
old canvases crumpled papers peanut butter sandwich
hanging from my back all my possessions as The Swat
Team breaks down the front door cause I'm behind
on my rent and The Land Lord come
to pay me a visit

yes I'm evicted convicted of being on the wrong side
and I'm convinced that this new state is taxation
without representation and I've watched this

new state force the 1st Amendment to
disappear and I've experienced the
protection of this new omnipotent
police state of by and for
    the rich

        yes I say it's high time
        to put on my wig
        and finally
        say
        goodbye

cause I Got a Lethal Dose of
        The Hound Dog Taylor Hunter S. Thompson
        Gimme Back My Wig
        I Gotta Get Out Of This Town Blues

copyright © 2007 Ron Whitehead

William McKeen, Professor and Chair
University of Florida, Department of Journalism
P.O. Box 118400, Gainesville, Florida 32611

12
hawk and crow

Ron at Tree Planting Ceremony, Louisville, Kentucky 2006
photo by Reginald J.K. Price

hawk and crow
alchemical sunrise prayer and meditation

dear Sarah, this is my morning prayer and meditation.
i do this every morning for us, for all and everything.
i love you, Ron

1.

all is well
all is well
all is well

peace and harmony

unity wholeness and love

i am empty
i am powerless
i surrender
i let go
now

i surrender my will
to God to God's will

i will fight no more forever

i surrender the story
i surrender the thinking
i surrender the drama
i surrender the soap opera

i surrender my will
to God to God's will

i surrender my will
to God to God's will

i will fight no more forever
i will fight no more forever

o spirit
o soul
embrace small self   ego
in emptiness openness and love

i am human
i am spirit
i am soul
and more
all one

as human and ego
i am broken
i suffer
i have been hurt
i have hurt
i am healed

letting go
all fear pain suffering
terror darkness
panic anxiety
doubt and death
letting go
letting go all jealousy
letting go all insecurity
letting go all fear
letting go

loving boundaries
loving thoughts actions expressions

unconditional love
unconditional love
unconditional love

forgiveness forgiveness forgiveness

thankful thankful thankful
choosing the good spiritual pathway
accepting and embracing all happiness and joy

failure
has been
my greatest
success
i am thankful for all my failures
i am thankful

my suffering has led me
to my healing
i am thankful for my suffering
i am thankful for my healing

i am healed
i am healed
i am healed

deeper and deeper and deeper

in the sanctuary
in the sanctuary
in the sanctuary

letting go all striving

letting go all striving
letting go all striving

sometimes necessary to go down
when climbing mountain
sometimes necessary to go down
when climbing mountain
sometimes necessary to go down
when climbing mountain

trusting the universe
trusting the universe
trusting the universe

healed completely

accepting and embracing unlimited
love gifts blessings and abundance

recognize refrain
relax resolve

guru rinpoche
your holiness the dalai lama
we are one

jesus christ
we are one

all ascended lightning masters
we are one

i am open to the wisdom
light and love
of the ra group

2.

accepting and embracing fearless
compassionate honesty
and self examination

don't know anything
beginner's mind
learning

listening waiting
being still
being patient

listening is
the greatest art of all
listening is
the greatest art of all
listening is
the greatest art of all

mindful awake aware
curious inquisitive
paying attention
coming to know
my whole self
completely

mindful mindful mindful

open mind
open heart
open to everything

openness
groundlessness

not grasping
not holding

lightening up
enlightened already

faith in higher power

no ideas
no opinions
no beliefs

courage patience
and faith in god in great spirit

loving compassionate wise
gentle and kind
caring considerate thoughtful

accepting and embracing
the eternal now
yes to present moment
fleeting memories

accepting and embracing
mystery paradox
uncertainty
not knowing

accepting and embracing
healing recovery rebirth
enlightenment
awakening to original being
original nature
to god's to great spirit's divine presence
in all and everything

right choices
weighing the consequences
knowing i can never have
all the information
i need and desire
accepting the outcome

healing all wounds
paying all debts
keeping all promises

letting go
all hope of fruition

letting go
all anger
resentment and blame
letting go

3.

the path
the steps
the sacred medicine place

hawk and crow

gnothi seauton
know thyself

god's great spirit's light and love
in all and everything

laughing and singing
rejoicing and cherishing
humor

forgiving
not judging
accepting

breathe in light
direct to heart
breathe out light
vast open heart
awakened heart
wounded heart
soft heart
loving heart
gentle heart
kind heart

4.

ancient father
sacred warrior
grandmothers
grandfathers
with us now
all one

in the turquoise sky chair

rise

as one
walk through
the lightning wall
and enter

the upper chamber
of the golden pyramid
levitate
over the open gemfilled sarcophagus
and through the crystal tip
of the pyramid
beams god's great holy spirit's universal creative light
we are one

unlimited abundance
unlimited abundance
unlimited abundance

spiritual alchemy
spiritual alchemy
spiritual alchemy

healed healed healed

5.

dear god o great universal spirit

we thank you thank you thank you
we love you and bless you

we thank you
for this beautiful day
for our lives
and for the opportunity
to grow in your love

we thank you for all
the gifts and blessings
you bestow upon us

we pray that you fill us
with the holy spirit
that we be pure channels
of your light and love
and truth and energy and blessings and creativity
uplifting and inspiring
all we come in contact with
comforting those who suffer
awakening all and everything
to your divine presence
in all and everything

dear god o great spirit
we pray that you bless
our love our marriage
we pray that you bless
our home
our beautiful treehouse apartment
we pray that you bless

our trucks and bicycles
our transportation
we pray that you bless
our creative work and our teachings
our poems stories songs and talks
we pray that you bless
us with abundant right livelihood income
from seen and unseen
known and unknown
expected and unexpected sources
from our creative work and our teachings
so we pay all our bills
all our debts
and live our dreams
we pray that you bless
my children my grandchildren
our families friends allies guides and angels
seen and unseen
we pray that you bless
our enemies

dear god o great spirit
we pray that your will be done
in all and everything
this and every day
now and forevermore

om

ron whitehead
july 25, 2007
aha, kentucky

13
epilogue

Ron & Sarah, Ohio County Kentucky, 2005, photo by Velvet Woosley

Sorrow, Moving On

last poem for Sarah

"what's for you will find you."
        Belfast saying

four years
the happiest
of my life

now
sorrow   blue bells   chime   sunset
night falls   moving on

strong
wounded heart
will heal
quickly

light
as a feather
moving on

releasing
the past
the future

releasing
all and everything
the now

releasing
sorrow, moving on
with joy

goodbye
thank you bougainvillea purple sunrise
good journey moving on

Sarah & Ron, Magic Gateway, 2007, photo by Christian Hansen

Ron Whitehead photo by Jeremy Hogan

Ron Whitehead is poet, writer, editor, publisher, organizer, scholar, professor. The son of Edwin and Greta Whitehead, he grew up on a farm outside of Centertown, population 323, in Ohio County, western Kentucky. He graduated from Ohio County High School in 1968. He attended Georgetown College, Western Kentucky University, The University of Lousville, and Oxford University (England). As undergraduate and graduate student he was the recipient of numerous scholarships, grants, fellowships, awards, and prizes including The Dean's Graduate School Citation at UofL and The English Speaking Union's Oxford Scholar Award plus the Joshua B. Everett Oxford Scholar Award. At Oxford he studied with Dr. Valentine Cunningham, Head of English Literature, at Oxford's International Graduate School. As poet and writer he is the recipient of numerous state, national, and international awards/prizes including The All Kentucky Poetry Prize and The Yeats Club of Oxford's Prize for Poetry. In 2004 he was inducted into Ohio County High School's Hall of Fame. In 2006 Dr. John Rocco (NYC) nominated Ron for The Nobel Prize in Literature.

Ron has taught college for 16 years at The University of Louisville, Spalding University, Jefferson Community College, St. Catharine College, and Bellarmine University. He has presented numerous talks, lectures, and writing workshops around the world at colleges, universities, and institutions which include Trinity College (Dublin, Ireland), The University of Iceland (Reykjavik, Iceland), The University of Braga (Braga, Portugal), The University of Nijmegen (Nijmegen, The Netherlands), New York University (New York, New York), Hofstra University (New York, New York), University of Louisville (Louisville, Kentucky), University of New Orleans (New Orleans, Louisiana), and many more. He has presented papers and chaired sessions at over 60 national and international Literature, Culture, and Arts Conferences including the Thirteenth Annual James Joyce Symposium at University College and Trinity College in Dublin, Ireland and the Eighty-Second Annual Scandinavian Culture Conference at Hofstra University on Long Island in New York.

In 1992 Ron founded **The Global Literary Renaissance**, a non-profit organization, supporting the global literary community. He was Director of the Global Literary Renaissance for 14 years. Ron has produced over 1,000 music and poetry events throughout Europe and the USA including many 24, 48, 72 & 90 hour Non-Stop Music & Poetry **INSOMNIACATHON**s plus he produced The Hunter S. Thompson Tribute (featuring Hunter, Johnny Depp, Warren Zevon, Roxanne Pulitzer, David Amram, Hunter's mother, Virginia, & son, Juan, & many others), the London International Poetry & Song Festival (with Richard Deakin), The New York City Underground Music & Poetry Festival (with Casey Cyr & others), The Netherland's 10-day International Meer Dan Woorden Festival (with Jan Pankow & others), LIVE at THE RUD Benefit Concert (with Jim James and Sarah Elizabeth), plus many many more.

He has edited over 1,000 titles and published over 600 titles including work by His Holiness The Dalai Lama, President Jimmy Carter, Seamus Heaney, Jack Kerouac, Diane di Prima, Allen Ginsberg, John Updike, BONO, Yoko Ono, Andy Warhol, Amiri Baraka, Rita Dove, David Amram, Thomas Merton, Wendell Berry, Edvard Munch, William S. Burroughs, Hunter S. Thompson, Lawrence Ferlinghetti, Gregory Corso, Herbert Huncke, James Laughlin, Douglas Brinkley, Lee Ranaldo, Robert Hunter, Anne Waldman, Ed Sanders, David Minton, Bob Holman, Cathal O'Searcaigh, Eithne Strong, Theo Dorgan, Jim Carroll, Casey Cyr, Denis Mahoney, Frank Messina, Steve Dalachinsky, Jean Genet, Jan Kerouac, Christopher Felver, Brother Patrick Hart, Robert Lax, and many many others. Ron recently retired from editing, publishing, and organizing events.

Ron's work has been exhibited round the world from New York City to

Louisville to New Orleans to San Francisco and from India to Czech Republic to Italy to Portugal to Ireland to The Netherlands to Iceland and beyond. The UN/UNESCO "Poetry On The Peaks" program selected The Dalai Lama/Ron Whitehead "Never Give Up" message/poem poster as its theme for 2002. Thousands of copies were donated and shipped to cities, mountain villages, Buddhist, and other, communities, groups, and organizations round the world. The "Never Give Up" poem has been published in numerous publications including NATIONAL GEOGRAPHIC, a book by His Holiness The Dalai Lama, and many others.

For the past 17 years Ron has been GOing non-stop. He is the author of 18 books and he has work on over 20 CDs.

His BOOK titles include:
WESTERN KENTUCKY: Lost & Forgotten, Found & Remembered (with Sarah Elizabeth)
THE THIRD TESTAMENT: Three Gospels of Peace (all 3 previously published Hozomeen Press books revised/edited in one volume with art by Lawrence Ferlinghetti & David Minton)
BEAVER DAM ROCKING CHAIR MARATHON (books 1 & 2 new revised 3rd edition)
EVE & THE OPHIDIANS
EXTERMINATE NOISE (with Charlie Newman)
GROUND ZERO
NOT-KNOWING (with Libby Ackerman)
LOVE and DEATH (with David Minton)
QUEST FOR SELF IN THE OCEAN OF CONSCIOUSNESS: IBSEN, HAMSUN, MUNCH, JOYCE: THE ORIGINS OF MODERNISM & EXPRESSIONISM

His CD titles include:
TAPPING MY OWN PHONE
KENTUCKY ROOTS
KENTUCKY: poems, stories, songs (with Sarah Elizabeth)
KENTUCKY BLUES (with David Amram)
I WILL NOT BOW DOWN (with Icelander Michael Pollock)
EXTERMINATE NOISE (with Charlie Newman)
NOT MUTE
FROM ICELAND TO KENTUCKY & BEYOND
OFF THE CUFF
SWAN BOATS @ FOUR (with Paul K)
THE SHAPE OF WATER (with James Walck)
THE VIKING HILLBILLY APOCALYPSE REVUE

3 SHOTS of THE VIKING HILLBILLY APOCALYPSE REVUE
CLOSING TIME

Ron reads his work with musicians from around the world, in all genres of music, including David Amram, Iceland's Sigur Ros, Tyrone Cotton, Iceland's Michael & Danny Pollock of The Outsiders, Jim James of My Morning Jacket, Paul K & The Weathermen, Lee Ranaldo of Sonic Youth, Frank Messina & Octopoet & Spoken Motion, James Walck & The Mind2Hands Symphonia, Vassar Clemens, Tom House, By The Grace of God, Black Pig Liberation Front, Jeremy Podgursky & The Pennies, Blowup in Japanese, RB Morris & Hector Qirko, Scaramongo, Sarah Elizabeth, Tony Redhouse, & numerous others. His groups have included Voices Without Restraint, Ron Whitehead's Apocalypse Jam, and The Viking Hillbilly Apocalypse Revue. He and Sarah Elizabeth perform together and tour constantly. Ron's Published in Heaven CD, **CLOSING TIME**, and his Published in Heaven book, **THE THIRD TESTAMENT: Three Gospels of Peace** were released in 2005. He was recently nominated for the Nobel Prize in Literature by New York City professor, James Joyce scholar, music critic, and author of many books, Dr. John Rocco.

To The Nobel Prize Committee,

I am writing you about one of America's greatest poets. His name is Ron Whitehead and for his entire career he has written volatile and important verse that has given a new presence to American poetry. Whitehead's work is in the tradition of the Beat Generation but also deeply influenced by rock and roll, the legacy of the European avant-garde from Knut Hamsun to James Joyce, and his own native Kentucky. He is at the same time a regional and universal writer; Kentucky is his home but the world is his subject. Whitehead's poetry is a powerful summation of the American spirit.

I would like to take this time to bring this extraordinary poet to your attention for consideration for the Nobel Prize in literature. Whitehead's poetry is exuberant and shocking, delicate and blunt, combative and sensitive. There is a vital spirituality in his work that questions the nature of artistic creativity at the same time it embodies it. His work is profoundly engaged in critiquing the control modern American culture has over the individual and the planet. *The Beaver Dam Rocking Chair Marathon* is a summation of his aesthetics: part Bildungsroman, part rock protest, all Whitehead white hot poetic energy.

As the profile in this package indicates, Whitehead is a tireless promoter of poetry and its power to heal the world. To recognize his work is to recognize the power of the word to resist imperialism, intolerance, and hate. Whitehead has made American poetry a vehicle for social change and a power to transform the world...

Thank you for considering this important American writer.

Yours sincerely,

Dr. John Rocco

Associate Professor of Humanities
SUNY (State University of New York Maritime)

James Joyce scholar John Rocco is the author of *The Nirvana Companion, The Beastie Boys Companion, The Doors Companion, The Grateful Dead Companion,* and other Schirmer Books. He is completing a volume on James Joyce. His novel *Fur* was released in 2005. He is a critic for *American Book Review* and numerous other literary and music publications.

Several thousand of Ron's works have been published round the world in a diverse range of publications from TRIQUARTERLY (Northwestern University/Illinois) to ARTFORUM (Czech Republic) to BLUE BEAT JACKET (Japan) to BEAT SCENE (England) to SOUTHERN REVIEW (North Carolina).

Ron has presented over 5,000 readings of his own creative work round the world.

"Can poems and stories matter? Make a difference? Ron Whitehead believes so. Ron Whitehead is one of those ancient poets who were and are prophets. He sees injustice and directs us back to the path of justice. His poems and stories blend the terrible beauty of the natural world with questions of global social conscience. For Ron life is a quest to grow his soul. Ron is a non-violent spiritual warrior who, regardless of the consequences, fights for freedom and equal rights for all. His poems and stories defy categorization. They are original."

Ron's work is in museum, library, and private collections around the world. The University of Louisville Rare Books & Archives is the permanent repository for Ron's work (past, present, future). 1,500 pieces (of thousands) have been catalogued. Four exhibits have been held. A major exhibition, with catalog, is being planned.

For the past 4 years Ron and **Sarah Elizabeth** performed toured presented their work across the USA and Europe. Ron and Sarah's new co-authored book, **WESTERN KENTUCKY: Lost & Forgotten, Found & Remembered**, was released in 2006.

In 2006 Sarah landed the lead role in RED VELVET CAKE, an independent feature film produced in Kentucky. Ron co-wrote the screenplay. The film will, hopefully, premiere in the fall of 2007 or 2008.

In 2007 Ron & Sarah are busier than ever working on new recording, writing, performance, and film projects. They recently returned from performances, seminars, visits, and travels in Portugal. As soon as they returned from Portugal they left for The Wanderer Tour: From New York & Kentucky to California & Beyond: with Frank Messina, Tyrone Cotton, Andy Cook, & Christian Hansen. During the spring Ron's I WILL NOT BOW DOWN cd was #1 on northern California radio (www.kmud.org). His "Tapping My Own Phone" won Best Spoken Word track in NYC's People's Choice Awards. 2007 will see the release of Sarah's new DON'T DIE YET CD (September 4th); a new Ron Whitehead & Frank Messina, legendary NYC poet, & New York Mets' Poet Laureate, cd, WALKING HOME (September release); a new book by Ron, THE WANDERER (October); Ron's new I REFUSE cd (October); plus USA and Europe performances. Ron is included in Christopher Felver's beautiful new book, BEAT (Last Gasp Press). September 8th Ron performed at NYC's Annual HOWL Festival. October 20th Ron and Sarah will celebrate the release of 3 new CDs and 1 new book with a concert at The Kentucky Center for The Arts. The concert will also feature Frank Messina and Tyrone Cotton. October 27th thru 30th Ron and Sarah perform at LIPS 2, The London International Poetry & Song Festival. From May 1st to June 30th, 2008 The Wanderer Ron Whitehead Europe Tour. Ron will perform in Iceland, The Netherlands, Belgium, France, England, Scotland, Ireland, Portugal, Italy, and Greece.

When not traveling Ron lives in Kentucky. His official website, www.tappingmyownphone.com, annually receives over one million hits from more than 65 countries.